# PRELUDE TO

GW00788541

# CONTENTS

# INTRODUCTION

This year sees the 50th anniversary of the outbreak of World War Two. The preceding months were a period of hurried preparation for the coming onslaught and the airfield personnel in Kent knew that they would bear the brunt of any attacks and attempted landings by the enemy. Kent became known as Hell Fire Corner during 1940 but much of the early preparation during 1938 and 1939 gave the county a fighting chance. The contents of this book give a description of just some of that preparation.

Robin J. Brooks

Biggin Hill: the last Empire Air Day, 1939. The new aircraft types on display include an H.P. Harrow, Fairey Battle, Hawker Hurricane and Airspeed Oxford. A 32 Squadron Gloster Gauntlet II, KT-P can also be seen.

(A. Thomas)

## Chapter 1

# BIGGIN HILL 1938 – 1939

### By Len Pilkington

In September 1938 when Mr Chamberlain flew to Munich for the meeting with the German Chancellor, Herr Hitler, to most people the threat of war due to the trouble in Europe was now a reality and the meeting a delaying tactic to give time to organise for the conflict ahead.

Our story of the year September 1938 – September 1939 at Biggin Hill must be prefaced for clarity by a brief account of the research and development and activities carried out at Biggin Hill in the previous seven years. The airfield reopened after an expansion programme in 1932 and now became a two squadron fighter station housed in the North Camp, with the Army occupying the South Camp, its School of Anti-Aircraft Defence researching and developing the latest advances in gunnery, searchlights and other aircraft detection techniques.

In 1936, with Europe in turmoil and trouble in other parts of the world where aircraft were used increasingly to bomb cities, the term 'the bomber will always get through' was a reality and therefore an effective method of early detection was urgently required. Britain had the fighters, top class in their day, but unless they could intercept the enemy quickly and early they were ineffective.

In 1936 Biggin Hill became part of the new Fighter Command and it was selected as the controlling airfield of 'C' Sector, Number 11 Group, comprising the airfields of West Malling, Gravesend, Hawkinge and Manston.

A team headed by Squadron Leader Ragg, a navigation expert, visited Biggin Hill to develop an effective method of aircraft interception. Originally planned for three days their work took considerably longer, but they succeeded, and developed a simple but highly effective method of aircraft interception known as the 'Principle of Equal Angles'. The enemy aircraft were located by the new R.D.F. System (later known as Radar) and fighters were guided by radio to an interception point based on this principle.

Our story now resumes in August 1938. In residence were 32 and 79 Squadrons with Gloster Gauntlet II in the North Camp and the School of Anti-Aircraft Defence in the South Camp. On 5th August Biggin Hill was brought to 'immediate readiness for war'. RAF and Army personnel on leave were recalled; reservists, auxiliaries and territorials were called-up and the fighter squadrons put on standby. To augment the squadrons at Biggin Hill 601 (Auxiliary) Squadron's Hawker Demons flew in from Northolt and all squadrons

3

Biggin Hill 1938. 32 Squadron air exercises. Pilots at dispersal in front of a Gloster Gauntlett II. (Air Commodore P.M. Brothers)

4

Biggin Hill 1939. A 32 Squadron Hurricane I is refuelled for a night flying exercise.

were put to 'available' — Germany had marched into the Sudetenland. The state of readiness lasted until 30th September when Mr Chamberlain returned from Munich and landed at Heston proclaiming 'Peace in our time'.

Life as it was, however, did not return to Biggin Hill. The reservists and territorials returned to civilian life, but they now reported for one or two evenings a week for training. One squadron was always 'available' and the airfield prepared for the conflict to come. The beautiful silver aircraft were camouflaged in drab green and brown and by November the Gauntlets had been replaced by Hurricanes equipped with the latest VHF radios, and 32 and 79 Squadrons were joined for a few months of combined training by Hurricanes of 3 Squadron who flew in from Kenley. November also saw a change in command, Wing Commander Lock being replaced by Wing Commander Grice.

The face of the airfield was also changing, buildings were painted for camouflage and the whole physical appearance of the airfield was altered by painting roads and hedges on the grass. Trenches and deep shelters were dug and the buildings were sandbagged. It is interesting to note that the Luftwaffe target map and photos accompanying this article issued 16th February 1939 still show the aircraft landing circle.

On the Army side Major H.E. Harrison with the School of Anti-Aircraft Defence recalls the training of service and territorial army personnel in the use of sound location, searchlights and anti-aircraft gunnery, but at the outbreak of war most units moved to Shrivenham, leaving the Army responsible for the

School of Anti-Aircraft Defence. Combined instructors of Biggin Hill and Gosport SAAD before moving to Shrivenham.
(Major H. Harrison)

defence of the airfield. In April the Cabinet sought powers to call up territorial army anti-aircraft units for full time defence and this followed soon after.

Captain D.B. Goodchild, with the 34th Battalion, Queen's Own West Kent Royal Engineers, Territorials, 336 Company, Blackheath, was called up to Biggin Hill in the Munich Crisis of 1938, released and later recalled to Biggin Hill in July 1939 and served in the operations room as Army (Royal Artillery) attached to the RAF.

In the operations room RAF and Auxiliary Air Force controllers were trained in the latest techniques of controlling the fighters at their disposal at Biggin Hill and the other sector airfields, and Army and territorials trained alongside in co-ordinating AA, searchlights, etc. The operations room in which the controllers worked was situated in the operations block, a reinforced concrete building above ground situated across the road from the station headquarters.

The main feature of the room was a large glass screen dividing the room, upon which was superimposed a map of 'C' Sector encompassing an area of Kent and Sussex from Biggin Hill to the South Foreland in the east and Biggin to Eastbourne to the south. Plots of our own aircrafts' position represented by rubber stickers were marked on the screen. On a large table bearing a map of Southern England, tilted to give a better view to the RAF and Army controllers situated in a raised balcony, were placed plots of enemy aircraft, the information fed in by the operations room of Number 11 Group, Uxbridge.

The technique of raider interception based on the 'Principle of Equal Angles' relied on information supplied by the radar stations along the coast and visual sightings by the Observer Corps. This was fed to the Filter Room at Fighter Command HQ, Bentley Priory where the accuracy of the reports was assessed and, if thought to be genuine, passed to 11 Group HQ control room at Uxbridge. The appropriate sector would then be selected to deal with the raid. The operation worked very well and exercises based on this were conducted by 32 Squadron Gauntlets on many unsuspecting civil airliners crossing the coast.

The coming of the winter snows restricted flying at Biggin Hill but the spring brought rehearsals for the coming annual Empire Air Day display on 20th May. On this day sixty-two service and sixteen civilian aerodromes opened their gates to the public. This year the event held a particular significance as it marked the coming of age of the RAF and with the threat of war in the air people were anxious to see the latest in air defence.

At Biggin Hill the attendance figures broke all records. The 'Kentish Times' reported that over 20,000 people watched a highly skilled display of flying and that before the programme started at 2 p.m. all roads from London were blocked. Before the display commenced the Secretary of State for Air, Sir Kingsley Wood, accompanied by his Parliamentary Secretary, Sir Edward Campbell, Member for Bromley, arrived at Biggin Hill to be greeted by Air Chief Marshall Sir Cyril Newall and Mr Edward Melville, Secretary to the Chief of Air Staff, before boarding a DH Rapide for a tour of some of the other airfields. Sir Kingsley was to return later in the day.

Blenheims IF of 601 Squadron with ventral gun packs, flew in to Biggin Hill September 1939 to augment 32 and 79 Squadrons.                                                        (RAF Museum)

At 2 p.m. promptly·a Biggin Hill Hurricane opened the flying with a fine display of aerobatics whilst below the Station Commander, Wing Commander R. Grice, inspected units of the local Air Defence Cadet Corps (later the ATC). A skilled display of glider flying by Mr E.J. Furlong was followed by a blast on the station siren which scrambled a squadron of Hurricanes standing by to ward off a bomber attack from the west. Four Hurricanes then proceeded to bomb a canvas model of a ship. On the ground a sobering demonstration of decontamination after a gas attack was carried out by members of the Beckenham ARP.

The afternoon progressed with displays by Gladiators, a large flight of Ansons from Manston, Sunderland and Stranraer flying boats and a Lysander, but the highlight of the afternoon was a spectacular display of aerobatics by a special works Hurricane flown by a company test pilot, Flight Lieutenant Richard Reynall. To demonstrate the effectiveness of the AA defences a drogue towed by a Hawker Henley was fired upon by the gunners.

As evening approached Sir Kingsley Wood returned to the aerodrome in the Air Council Rapide and on landing was met by the Station Commander, Wing Commander R. Grice. Sir Kingsley, accompanied by the Station Commander, then proceeded to inspect units of the RAF and Army, the RAFVR, AAF, Territorials and the newly formed Civil Air Guard, Air Defence Cadet Corps and Beckenham ARP personnel. To end such a memorable day Sir Kingsley addressed the crowd over the loudspeakers and finished a stirring speech by announcing that over a million people attended the displays throughout the country.

Another regular event was the Annual Air Exercises this year held in conjunction with the Air Defence of Great Britain, much bigger than before, from 8 p.m. on 8th August to 7 p.m. on 11th August. 'Flight Magazine' reported that over 1,300 machines took part, along with units of the Territorial Army AA divisions, the London Balloon Barrage and the Observer Corps. The area of the country involved a line from south and east of Withersea, Macclesfield, Droitwich, Hungerford, Salisbury and Bournemouth known as 'Westland' and an imaginary enemy, 'Eastland', situated somewhere across the North Sea.

The object of the exercise was for the 'Westland' forces to defend Great Britain against the bomber attacks of 'Eastland' and for realism blackout conditions at night would prevail. 'Westland' defences totalled 500 fighters out of a total of 800 aircraft and many service aerodromes in the area participated. Biggin Hill provided four squadrons for the exercise, three of Hurricanes and one of fighter Blenheims, three squadrons being available during daylight and one at night. On Tuesday 8th and Wednesday 9th, Biggin Hill squadrons were very busy intercepting twenty-four 'Eastland' raids but from mid-day Wednesday until Thursday low cloud, rain and mist put an end to further operations.

With the Air Exercises over, Biggin Hill aircraft often flew hazardous night operations, often to check the effectiveness of the blackout. During one of these exercises 32 Squadron tragically lost two aircraft and pilots in one night. Air Commodore Peter Brothers was a Flight Lieutenant with 32 Squadron at Biggin Hill during 1938/39 and recalls . . . 'September 1938, Memories of Colour Hoisting Parades at 8 a.m., prayers followed by the Station Commander's inspection and 32 and 79 Squadrons marching off to their hangars. As we pilots made our way to the Pilots' Room came the shout 'Man the doors' and the ground crew responding, hangar doors rolling open and our Gloster Gauntlets wheeled out and lined up on the tarmac wing tip to wing tip.

'As detailed by our two Flight Commanders, we would be airborne shortly after 9 a.m. for formation or air attack practice, air firing, or interception of other aircraft, as required and be back in the Pilots' Room for coffee by 10.45. At 12.30 we retired to the mess for lunch returning at 2 p.m. until tea at 4.30. On rare occasions we would manage two flights in the morning or one in the afternoon, but the latter period was mostly spent servicing the aircraft for the morrow.

'There would be time for tennis or squash before drinks at 7.30 and dinner at 8.00, Tuesdays being Guest Nights, attendance compulsory. Mondays, Thursdays and Fridays also required Mess Dress but Wednesdays were informal as it was sports afternoon.

'As our re-equipment with Hurricanes commenced, so did the Munich Crisis brew and our pleasantly ordered life temporarily ended. We were ordered to a high state of readiness, sleeping in tiered bunks in the Pilots' Room beside our flying clothing lockers. Came the night we were ordered to 'Cockpit Readiness with engines running'! It was so wet and foggy that we could hardly find the aircraft. We were not amused. The next night we were asleep under orders to man the cockpits at 4 a.m. when the Duty Officer shook each of us awake to tell us orders were cancelled and we could go back to sleep. We were even less amused.

'The crisis over, life returned almost to normal, but we relished the fresh sense of urgency which brought us more flying on our new Hurricanes, always two and often three sorties a day with more emphasis on night flying. The latter brought new problems, compounded during 'blackout' exercises when there were no local lights, for the flames and glare from the twin exhausts created difficulties in seeing ahead and down, particularly when practising landings by the light of our single port headlamp which in any case shone at an angle to the left rather than directly ahead.

'It was during one of these night landings that I inadvertently flew through the top of a tree and landed festooned with branches and with the radiator stuffed with leaves. One tragic night, when a belt of low cloud lay in the valley adjacent to the airfield, cost us the lives of two pilots: Pilot Officer 'Young' Olding who flew into rising ground and Flight Lieutenant Robin Buchanan-Wollaston, who was dropping flares to help us locate him.

'But we were young and resilient and did not dwell on such misfortunes. Time could always be found to visit the 'White Hart' at Brasted, our 'local', and other diversions from routine such as aerobatic displays on Empire Air Day, Annual Air Defence Exercises and the use of our aircraft for weekend visits to friends and relations, considered beneficial in developing initiative and resourcefulness because one had no outside support.

'Whilst we took our flying duties seriously and strove for efficiency, it was a relaxed and happy period. When it ended with the outbreak of war on September 3rd we had in reserve the energy necessary to cope with the stress and strains of the Battle of Britain . . .

'On 24th August general mobilisation of reservists once again took place and men were recalled from leave. 601 Squadron Blenheims equipped in the fighter role, with ventral machine gun packs, flew in to augment the Hurricanes of 32 and 79 Squadrons.

'Just after Mr Chamberlain had announced we were at war at 11 a.m. on 3rd September, the air raid sirens sounded. At Biggin Hill three Hurricanes of 32 Squadron scrambled. In this event it proved a false alarm but soon they were to be tested to the full and to prove that Biggin Hill was indeed "The Strongest Link" in the chain of airfields that ringed the defences of London.'

My thanks to the following for their help:
Air Commodore P.M. Brothers, CBE, DSO, DFC
Major H.E. Harrison, MBE
Captain D.B. Goodchild
'Flight' Magazine
'Kentish Times'

## Chapter 2

# No. 20 ELEMENTARY & RESERVE FLYING TRAINING SCHOOL — GRAVESEND

### By Ray Munday

The Royal Air Force Volunteer Reserve existed to provide for the continued flying practice of pilots who had completed their term of full-time service in the RAF and were now posted to the Reserve List. It was also expanded in time of need to train civilian men to fly to provide the reserves that the RAF would need in a war.

The formation of No.20 ERFTS at Gravesend Airport was announced locally in the 'Gravesend Reporter' issue of 25th September 1937. The announcement stated that Airports Limited, the owners of both Gravesend and Gatwick Airports, had obtained a contract from the Air Ministry for the school to be opened at Gravesend on 1st October 1937. Flight Lieutenant J.B. Tatnall was to be the Officer in Charge and he would have six permanent flying instructors, together with six de Havilland Tiger Moth and six Hawker Hart training aircraft. The training would commence on the Tiger Moths and progress to the Harts. The school duly opened on the prescribed date with a full complement of instructors and aircraft, together with fourteen pupils.

The pupils, all volunteers, had to be educated to School Certificate standard and be between the ages of 18 and 25 years. They joined initially for a period of five years and all were sworn in as Sergeant Pilots, although promotion to higher ranks would be available to some of them later on. Their obligations were to report immediately in time of war, to attend for training regularly and to go into the air whenever ordered to do so, all for the princely sum of 10 shillings per day (50 new pence) whilst training and 12 shillings and sixpence (62½ new pence) per day when trained.

The trainees attending at civilian airfields were not expected to wear uniform but were supplied with a one-piece flying suit at the airfield. When the weather was not suitable for flying, classroom work on the theory of flight, engines, navigation, signals, armament, rigging, airmanship and administration took place in the airport buildings. Later, as more pupils were taken on, time spent in the air was at a premium even with more aircraft, so courses would be in the air and in the classroom according to a rota. This necessitated the training aircraft being flown almost continually during daylight hours and attention to the condition and serviceability of the aircraft was most important. Important regulations and

A Royal Navy Air Arm Course and Instructors at 20 ERFTS Gravesend 1939. 3rd from the left is F/O Matthews, 4th F/O Kirchner and 6th from left F/Lt. Tatnall, Officer in Charge of the School.

(S. Parsonson)

Hawker Audax K7418 after a landing accident at 20 ERFTS Gravesend on 7th May 1938. It was written off in this accident. (S. Parsonson)

duties were placed on staff at the airport to ensure that no aircraft ran short of fuel whilst in the air. With the need to keep the aircraft flying, it was all too easy to forget to refuel.

As the training continued and the prospect of war in Europe drew ever closer, the need to train more pilots caused Airports Limited to announce in 'Flight' magazine on 14th April 1938, that the Air Ministry had increased the strength of 20 ERFTS by five more aircraft and one full-time flying instructor. Further expansion came about when pupils from the Air Branch of the Royal Navy commenced their flying training at the airport. As available space was all but taken up the Royal Navy trainees were brought to the airport each day by motor coach from the Royal Naval College at Greenwich. The available hangar space had also been taken up by this time so several 'Bessoneaux' canvas hangars were erected to protect the mainly wood and fabric aircraft from the elements. The White Ensign was now flown from the airport's flagpole to indicate the presence of the Royal Navy.

In March 1939 the flying instructors at the school numbered fifteen. Flight Lieutenants Tatnall, Le Good, Johnson and Nugent, Flying Officer Noblston together with the civilian pilots Messrs Elliot, Rathbone and Willis, taught the RAFVR pupils. Flying Officers Kirchner, Spanton, Oliver, Matthews and Higgins assisted by Messrs Hymans and Jameson, taught the Navy to fly. The flying hours, in suitable weather, were basically from 9 a.m. until 5 p.m. or sunset,

Hawker Audax K7415 waits for take off at 20 ERFTS Gravesend in 1938. Tiger Moths of the School in the background. This aircraft was destroyed on 9th April 1939 when F/O Sciortino crashed between Shoreham and Eynsford. (S. Parsonson)

A line up of 12 de Havilland Tiger Moths of 20 ERFTS in front of the 'Bessoneaux' hangars in 1939. (S. Parsonson)

whichever came later, and on Saturdays from 9 a.m. until 12.15 p.m.; the training sessions being split into 90 minute periods.

With so much activity going on at the airport, it was almost inevitable that there would be accidents, but luckily most were of a minor nature, although the damaged aircraft obviously meant that valuable training time was lost whilst repairs were carried out by the staff at the airport. On Friday afternoon of 21st January 1938, Mr J.F. Carroll was forced to crash land in Hawker Audax K7416, when he hit some trees whilst flying in low cloud in the Maplescombe Valley near Farningham. The aircraft was written off when it finished upside down after the crash landing. Mr Carroll was lucky enough to walk away from the crash uninjured. Three fatal accidents occurred in 1939, the first on 9th April. Flying Officer B.J. Sciortino aged 24 of the Reserve was killed whilst practising aerobatics when he side-slipped near the ground and caught the wing tip of the aircraft on an oak tree at Romney Street Farm between Shoreham and Eynsford. The Hawker Audax K7415 was destroyed.

Worse was to follow the next month when in the afternoon of 12th May 1939, Flying Officer F.R. Spanton took up his pupil, Midshipman C.G. Hodgkinson, in Tiger Moth N5487 for an extra blind flying training flight. The rear cockpit of the Tiger Moth was fitted with a canvas hood on metal frames which enclosed the pupil completely, forcing him to fly relying solely on the instruments to keep the aircraft on course and at the correct height. The instructor sat in the front open cockpit and gave instructions to the pupil down a voice tube. Spanton had taken the Moth up to 1,000 feet and then gave control of the aircraft to Hodgkinson. He informed him of the height, course and speed to fly the aircraft. As the aircraft came in to land at Gravesend Airport from a southerly direction at about 400 feet, it collided with another Tiger Moth N6451 flown by Flying Officer F.R. Matthews, with Midshipman A. Taylor as his pupil. This aircraft was also carrying out a blind flying exercise with Taylor under the hood flying the same course and at the same height. Both aircraft crashed to the ground in Claylane Woods, just to the north of the A2 London to Rochester road. Spanton was killed instantly, Matthews died later. Taylor was only slightly hurt but Hodgkinson was seriously injured. He was attended by Dr Maxwell Landau, the official Doctor to the School, and taken to Gravesend Hospital where his right leg was amputated. He later also had his left leg amputated and, inspired by Douglas Bader the legless flying ace, he made a full recovery to operational flying and, like Bader, was shot down and spent the rest of his war in a German prisoner-of-war camp. After the war he described his life in a book 'Best Foot Forward' published in 1957 by Odhams Ltd.

At the subsequent RAF Inquiry, the blame for the collision was placed on Spanton as he was in charge of the overtaking aircraft. The 'Gravesend Reporter' in its account of the inquest, related how two days before the aircraft collision Spanton had been involved in a motoring accident in which a woman had been killed and that possibly his mind had been distracted by this whilst in the air. Both Spanton and Matthews were, by all accounts, excellent instructors and Matthews had earlier taught Amy Johnson, the famous airwoman, to fly.

Another fatality occurred on 25th June 1939, when 21-year-old Sgt. J.E. Morgan was killed when his Tiger Moth K4287 crashed at Rowhill Woods, Wilmington. The subsequent Court of Inquiry heard that Morgan, who had flown 22 hours solo, was sent out to practise spinning and steep turns and crashed whilst performing these at an altitude of 1,500 feet, instead of the prescribed 3,000 feet. The Inquiry was also told that Jones had perhaps been performing for onlookers on the ground, as his home was nearby at Crayford.

Training continued until late all through the summer of 1939 with the local staff at the airport working a shift system to deal with this. However, by 1st September 1939 when war was imminent, the School was disbanded at Gravesend Airport in anticipation of the airport being taken over completely by the RAF and being used by regular fighting aircraft.

The King and Queen with Oswald Short are welcomed by the employees.          (Shorts)

Their Majesties leave the Empire flying boat *Australia* .          (Northcliffe Newspapers)

## Chapter 3

# THE ROYAL VISIT TO SHORT BROTHERS

## By Robin J. Brooks

By 1938 Short Brothers of Rochester had turned full circle from a struggling firm in the early 1930s, very short of aircraft production orders, to a full-time manufacturing capacity. War was looming on the horizon and although 1938 saw Shorts producing the Empire class flying boats for civil purposes, its military counterpart, the Sunderland, was already in full production. With the Air Ministry placing an order for a long range, heavily armed, four engined monoplane flying boat, the tender from Short Brothers was accepted and the prototype boat took to the River Medway on 4th October 1937, its first flight being on the 16th of the same month under the control of John Lankester Parker. As history tells us, the Sunderland was a winner and gave stirling service, but it is not so well known that before its fame, it gained a Royal assent.

As the new year of 1939 dawned it became obvious to the military that time was running out and that re-armament must be a priority. The war machine was put into top gear and it became known that Royalty wished to play its part, however small, in helping the war effort. A series of tours was organised by the Royal household, one of them being that their Majesties should visit the flying boats and land planes that were being built by Messrs Short Brothers at Rochester. Both the King and the Queen had expressed an interest in the building of the aircraft and on 14th March 1939, their Majesties drove to Rochester and were welcomed by huge flag waving crowds. Driving on to the esplanade, they were welcomed by Mr Oswald Short and his fellow directors with their families together with local dignitaries. When the formal introductions were over, the King and Queen went into the Seaplane works to begin their tour with a welcome of cheering and handclapping by the employees.

With total war becoming even closer and every day being valuable in the re-armament stakes the factory suspended work for just one hour as the Royal party proceeded and saw an average day in the life of Short Brothers. Inspecting the interior of the Empire flying boat *Australia*, the King expressed wonder at how very luxurious they were. The Queen on the other hand inspected a Sunderland flying boat spending some time speaking to the men building it. Mr B. Penny, who was working in the Seaplane shop at that time recalled that 'this was a day to be remembered. With so many people wanting to catch a glimpse of the King and Queen, I still wonder how on earth the scaffolding around the aircraft did not collapse under the strain of so many cheering folk. I can honestly say at this period that Shorts was just one happy family despite the advancing war.'

Shorts' main seaplane erection shop in 1939. (Shorts)

The tour proceeded into the milling shop where the King and Queen watched most intently as Mr H.J.E. Piper operated a milling machine. It was explained to them that here the metal was trimmed to size ready to be used on one of the aircraft. The King insisted that he should be given the opportunity to operate the machine and, under supervision, he was able to set the milling lathe to take another metal grinder.

The next stop on the tour was outside to the slipway in order that a Sunderland could give a demonstration and flypast for their Majesties. In fact two aircraft were airborne and gave a most impressive display, Oswald Short explaining to them that the Sunderland was already in squadron service with No.230 at Singapore and No.210 at Pembroke Dock. It had gained the nickname of 'Flying Porcupine' on account of its strong defensive armament, a comment that amused both King and Queen.

As the two display aircraft landed on the River Medway and tied up, it was time for the Royal party to leave the esplanade and drive the short distance to the newly opened Rochester Airport where Shorts were starting to manufacture the Stirling, the first four engined bomber for the RAF. Although the prototype aircraft had yet to fly, a half scale model had flown to provide valuable data on

18

Empire flying boats under construction in 1939.                    (Shorts)
NB. G-ADHL is *Canopus* of the Mercury/Maia composite.

the aerodynamic and handling features of the design. Again, amid hand-clapping and cheering, the King and Queen were shown over the assembly works and met personally many of the employees, shaking their hands warmly.

The visit lasted well over an hour longer than was scheduled, such was the interest of their Majesties in the work of this great pioneering aircraft manufacturing company. Walking between columns of cheering workers, the Royal couple reached their car and said fond farewells to Oswald Short and his employees. With three cheers sounding in their ears, the King and Queen drove out of the factory gates, gone but never to be forgotten in the history of the company.

Both the Sunderland and Stirling gave excellent service throughout the war, the former only being retired from the RAF as late as May 1959. Though the visit could not have encouraged the potential of these aircraft, the boost to the work force at a very tense and busy period did, for six months later both aircraft went to war.

A line up of the Avro Ansons of 48 Squadron at Manston in 1938, prior to their posting to Eastchurch in September. In the background can be seen the new hangars erected to ease the accommodation problems for aircraft.
(RAF Museum P7114)

Chapter 4

# 'A HOST OF ANSONS'
# Royal Air Force, Manston, 1938 – 39

## By David G. Collyer

From January 1936 Manston had been the home of the School of Air Navigation which trained pilots and navigators for long-range maritime reconnaissance, equipped with the first twin-engined, retractable undercarriage monoplane to be introduced into service, the Avro Anson. The aerodrome had also been shared by 48 Squadron, also equipped with Ansons, and the local Royal Auxiliary Air Force squadron, 500 (County of Kent), which was also later re-equipped with the same type of aircraft. Manston had had to accommodate the personnel from the regular squadrons and the World War One vintage huts surrounding the parade ground were fully occupied, while the hangars on both sides of the aerodrome were crowded with aircraft. The accommodation for aircraft was eased somewhat by the erection of some new hangars on the Birchington side of the aerodrome in 1938, but until 48 Squadron was posted to Eastchurch in September 1938 some temporary accommodation had to be found for personnel in various ancillary buildings and even tents.

The Munich Crisis of September 1938 was reflected in the digging of trench shelters, the establishment of machine gun posts for airfield defence and the introduction of blackout and anti-gas precautions. The airfield and buildings were camouflaged and ammunition and bomb dumps set down, whilst aircraft were painted in brown and green camouflage, with yellow undersides for the training aircraft. So hurriedly were these measures introduced that the only camouflage paint in store for Fighter Command was at Manston, and Flight Lieutenant Tom Roland of 74 Squadron at Biggin Hill flew down in a Magister Trainer to collect a supply.

Another result of the worsening situation in Europe was that 500 Squadron was posted to Detling aerodrome, near Maidstone on 28th September, having become part of No.16 (General Reconnaissance) Group. One of those involved in the move was AC.2 Sean Carson:

'My main memory of being at Manston was that we were accommodated in some 1914-18 vintage huts, very crowded. I remember the move to Detling. The squadron's equipment was loaded into a fleet of three-ton lorries and we set off at night. We travelled the length of Sittingbourne, and the noise of the lorries must have wakened people up, because by the time my particular lorry came along, the roadsides were lined with cheering men and weeping women — they thought that we were off to war!'

Three Avro Anson Mk 1s of the School of Air Navigation on a training flight over Thanet in 1938, while still in their pre-Munich Crisis silver doped finish. (RAF Museum P1651)

Interior of one of the new concrete huts erected at Manston on an inspection day. Accommodation huts were open to the public at the Empire Air Day display in May 1939.
(Photo via Mr B. Wells)

Another person who was disturbed by the events of September 1939 was LAC Len Wallis:

'I had been posted to Manston in April 1938, after serving for five years in Egypt. This was my second visit to Manston, having been posted there as a raw recruit in 1930. I was married on 17th September 1930 and planned to spend my honeymoon at No.43 Seafield Road, Ramsgate. The first week of my honeymoon was interrupted by a recall to camp when Mr Chamberlain went to Munich and returned waving that little piece of paper. When things quietened down I was allowed to rejoin my wife and live out-of-camp again.'

Also based at Manston at this time was Jack Withers, who was a Flight Mechanic attached to 48 Squadron, and later to the School of Navigation:

'Every morning the Ansons were pushed out of 'X' hangar, the big one which used to stand where the new control tower is now. There were two of us Flight Mechanics to each aircraft, but after the School of Air Navigation was expanded we had between three and six Ansons to maintain.

'The pilots used to come over by van or lorry and take the Ansons up, and sometimes we mechanics would be given a trip in the aircraft. On one occasion I was given a flight by a certain pilot and he did a barrel roll; thankfully he told me to hang on to some of the struts inside the fuselage before he started it.

'While the aircraft were away we worked on repairs and maintenance, and after I was transferred to the School of Air Navigation, a new metal hangar was built which was used to accommodate some of the Ansons. I remember this hangar being built as I was the first one to sweep the floor!

'Alongside the hangar was a little hut and at break times we would pop over for a couple of cups of tea and a "wad" from "Taffy" who ran it, before getting back to work.

'Wednesday afternoons were "Sports Afternoons" at RAF Manston, and the station had a very good reputation for sports, our own swimming pool, water polo team, football team, etc. A group of us were very keen on athletics and so we formed an Athletics Club. Amongst the members was the son of a Dover dentist, Bill Meeks, who was Kent Javelin Champion, and we spent our time training on discus, javelin, running etc and thoroughly enjoyed ourselves.'

During the summer of 1938 members of the Observer Corps attended at Manston to practice aircraft recognition, height judging and height finding, while local Army Territorial anti-aircraft units and the members of the airfield's own local defence gunners also practiced with target aircraft.

'One of the sights we used to see on Wednesday afternoons, while we were doing our athletics training, was the De Havilland Queen Bee radio-controlled anti-aircraft target biplanes. We used to see them take off and I think that there were a couple of them based at Manston. They were painted yellow overall and on one occasion I understand that one of them was lost when it flew out of range of the rather limited radio control equipment.'

With so much activity it is not surprising that accidents occurred, not only to the aircraft, but also on occasions to personnel as well. Jack Withers recalls one particularly accident-prone mechanic:

A formation fly-past of Avro Ansons of the School of Air Navigation over Thanet, while practising for the Empire Air Day display in May 1939.                    (Photo via Mr B. Wells)

'The Anson had a pitot head mounted between the fuselage and the engine, but there was just enough room to walk to it between the propeller arc and the fuselage side. We had one armourer lad who was very keen, and on one occasion he forgot himself and made a dash out backwards and was struck on the head by the propeller and received a bad cut. He was in severe pain, so he was rushed off to The Brook Hospital at Woolwich, and was fortunate enough to survive. I met him again later, and he told me that he had had a couple more serious accidents during his service career — and that he was now working in a glass works!'

One of the peculiarities of RAF Manston was the Parade Ground, which had a dip in the middle as the ground underneath had been excavated for shelters in World War One, and incidentally these were used again during the Battle of Britain. Jack Withers remembers that this subsidence involved some adaptation when parades were held:

'The Parade Ground, or the 'Square' as we knew it, was used for drill and I recall that we were told that they could only march so many men on it at any one time as there were underground caverns below which had started to cave-in.

The Parade Ground certainly did slope and it went right down in places. When we had the large ceremonial parades the band was always allocated the position in the middle of the 'Square' as they were the lightest. At the Air Officer Commanding's visit of March 1938 we were all waiting for him to arrive, and when the signal was given that he was on his way over, the band struck up the tune 'Here Comes the Bogey Man' so we would be ready for his arrival.'

One of the highlights of the year was the annual Empire Air Day displays held in May, when the aerodrome was thrown open to the general public to look round the hangars, workshops, and watch the flying display. The Avro Ansons of the School of Aerial Navigation were the highlight of the display in May 1939, starting the whole programme by taking off in sub-flights at 2.30 p.m. After formating over the aerodrome for a mass flypast, they departed to fly down the coast to visit other RAF aerodromes, including Biggin Hill, before returning some two-and-a-quarter hours later. The modern equipment of the RAF was seen when three Hurricanes 'beat-up' the aerodrome at low level, in contrast with the sedate flypast of the old Vickers Virginia biplane bomber for a para-chute dropping demonstration. Manston's naval connection during World War One was not forgotten, a Sunderland flying boat and three Stranrear flying boats making flypasts while en route round the coast. The modern RAF bomber was represented by a Vickers Wellington 'heavy bomber', and the Bristol Blenheim night fighters of 600 Squadron were followed by an ancient Handley Page Henley biplane bomber. Two Fairey Battle 'light bombers', a Miles Magister training aircraft and a Westland Lysander Army Co-Operation aircraft completed the programme, before the Ansons finished with a 'low-level bombing attack' on the aerodrome.

The visitors could also partake in joy-riding in civilian aircraft from Ramsgate's Municipal Airport, or tour parts of the camp which were open to the public. These included the Technical Training School, with a display of equipment and demonstrations of acetylene welding, parachute packing and maintenance work, while at the swimming pool there was a water polo match against Dover. At the East Camp, the School of Air Navigation mounted a display of maps, charts and navigation instruments, together with equipment used in weather forecasting at the Meteorological Section. On the opposite side of the aero-drome the cookhouse, dining hall and airmen's living quarters were on display. Proceedings ended with the station band beating retreat on the Parade Ground at 6.30 p.m.

July 1939 saw the return of the Observer Corps for more practice and this month also witnessed the departure of the Officer Commanding, Group Captain W.V. Strugnell, M.C., to be replaced by Group Captain Grey. The summer months saw Manston play host to units of the Royal Auxiliary Air Force, 501 Squadron having recently been re-equipped with Hawker Hurricanes, together with 601 Squadron and the last to arrive was 616 Squadron which departed at the end of August without completing their full stay due to the declaration of the National Emergency. The first week of August saw Manston participating in the Annual Air Defence Exercises on 7th and 8th of the month, when various bombers and light bomber squadrons undertook simulated attacks on London and the South East, which was defended by fighter squadrons by both day and night. Despite the inclement weather the Air Ministry stated that the exercises had involved some 1,300 aircraft as well as anti-aircraft, balloon and Observer Corps units in a full scale rehearsal, for what turned out to be the real thing less than 12 months later.

On 1st September 1939, on declaration of the General Emergency, preparations were made for the evacuation of the School of Air Navigation to St Athan, Wales, together with part of the Technical Training School transport section. Personnel living outside the camp were once again ordered to 'live-in', machine gun posts were mounted and the full-scale airfield defence scheme brought into operation. Jack Withers remembers the fateful morning of 3rd September 1939:

'We all went over to the NAAFI to hear Chamberlain's broadcast on that Sunday morning, and then we were ordered to pack-up our kit almost immediately afterwards and were taken down to Ramsgate Goods Station yard, where a complete train was awaiting us and our equipment. Not all of the equipment could be accommodated on the train, so some of us had to stay behind and guard the Goods Shed against fifth columnists until we could follow on the following day.'

As a Stores Clerk, Len Wallis would remain at Manston, and this was a busy time for him and his colleagues, but not without a certain humour concerning the evacuation of the Ansons of the School of Air Navigation:

'When the war clouds were looming, the Ansons were ferried away, and it was always a joke in the stores that, before the war started some dozen or so aircraft were always grounded awaiting spares, but when they were flown away to safety, only one remained behind. We had been preparing for some time for this event, and all sorts of aircraft and engine spares were arriving with codes on the packing cases, which we were to discover later were the numbers of the fighter squadrons which were to be based at Manston for defence purposes.

'In addition to preparing aircraft, numerous air raid shelters were built around the camp of brick and wood, known to us as "molehills", they were all right for bomb blast, but a bomb that dropped on or near the entrance caught the whole thing ablaze.'

For a few days, Manston was almost bereft of aircraft after the mass exodus of the Ansons, but on 10th September the Hawker Hurricanes of 3 Squadron arrived and began to fly patrols from Manston — the aerodrome was ready for its Second World War.

Acknowledgements: Mr L. Wallis; Mr J. Withers: 'The 'History of RAF Manston'; 'Flight' magazine; 'Twenty One Squadron'; 'Kent's Own'.

Chapter 5

# THANET'S CIVIL AIR GUARD
# Ramsgate Municipal Airport, 1938 – 39

## By David G. Collyer

Interest in civil aviation in Thanet had been fostered during the 1920s and 1930s by John T. Huddlestone and members of the Ramsgate Municipal Corporation. As early as 1928, together with two friends, John Huddlestone had formed Thanet Aviation Limited to promote joy-riding and flying displays from a site at Nethercourt, with regular weekend air displays and visits by touring 'Flying Circuses' such as Alan Cobham's, C.W.A. Scott's and C.H. Barnard. A regular scheduled airliner service was started by Hillman's Airways between Maylands, near Romford, Southend, Ipswich to the Continent via Ramsgate.

Having obtained a seat on the Ramsgate Borough Council, John Huddlestone next proceeded to encourage the founding of a Municipal Airport for Thanet, but in the end it was only Ramsgate which went ahead with the scheme, establishing its own Ramsgate Municipal Airport on a new site at Rumfields, which was officially opened in July 1937, although the site had been leased to The Straight Corporation two years earlier. The Thanet Aero Club was registered in February 1936 and trained many local residents to fly under the instruction of Chief Flying Instructor John Banting, assisted by Cliff Gifford and Ken Clarke.

The Thanet Aero Club was not equipped with the usual collection of De Havilland DH.60 Moths, only having G-AAHU at first, instruction being given on Hornet Moth G-ADMM initially which was later joined by two more DH.87Bs, G-AFDT and G-AFEE. In 1937 three Miles Hawk Trainers G-AFET/U and G-AFEV were taken onto the strength due to the increased numbers of potential pilots under training. Maintenance of aircraft was undertaken, together with repairs to both club machines and privately owned machines, the Chief Engineer being Mr H. Pentecost, assisted by his second-in-command John Bray, and mechanics Mark Bateman, Ken Almond and Bob Avery.

In 1938 the Munich Crisis precipitated preparations already being made for a possible European conflict, part of which involved the expansion of the Royal Air Force with new aircraft of modern design being ordered, but these would need pilots. Mr Peter Beechey remembers the background to the scheme to provide this personnel:

'Air Commodore Chamier (Secretary General of the Air League) was a great patriot and he considered that things were in a "bit of a state", with the forces having been run down during the preceding decades. He could see what was

Bill Stone (right) and Ron Smith, march proudly along Ramsgate seafront in their Civil Air Guard uniforms after taking part in the local National Service Parade in June 1939.
(Photo via Mr W. Stone)

coming, and did everything he could to encourage people to learn to fly, and also to get a nucleus of trained pilots in case war came.'

A scheme was started, known as the Civil Air Guard, in co-operation with the established flying clubs to subsidise the initial training of civilian pilots:

'Anybody who joined the Civil Air Guard had to sign a promise that they would serve with the RAF in an emergency, if war came. For signing that promise, the Government subsidised the clubs, CAG members paying only 5/-per hour for flying instruction while the Government paid the rest. So doing it also helped the clubs as they were all in a pretty bad way and it helped them survive. For each pilot who qualified the club received a bounty of £25.00. I still have my log book with some CAG receipts for my flights which show "½ hr flying 2/6 (12½p)". You had a very smart flying suit, which I think you had to buy yourself, and when you had got your 'A' licence, you were entitled to put up a "dirty great pair of wings".'

The official date of the commencement of the Civil Air Guard scheme was 1st October 1938, but so keen was the response by potential trainees, that some clubs started earlier than the official date. One of the first batch to commence their training at Ramsgate was John Rootes who, together with some twenty other young men and women, started instruction under the direction of Squadron Leader E.C. Eckersley-Maslin, the Airport Manager. The instructors were John Dade, Tommy 'Tan' Forsythe and Tony Stewart, and the first entry in Mr Rootes' log book is for 20th October 1938 when he received 40 minutes dual instruction under John Dade. After some ten hours and twenty minutes dual instruction, John was able to enter:

'6th March 1939 DH87B G-ADMM nil hrs 5 mins SELF SOLO!'

However, this was only the start and there are further entries for both solo and dual instruction flights with John Dade and H.W. Banting, until 17th May 1939 when John took his test for his 'A' licence which would enable him to qualify as a pilot.

'The 'A' licence flying test consisted of performing three figures-of-eight between 1,000 and 2,000 feet without losing height, and then a gliding landing from 600 feet without power on to a ground marker. (There was also an oral test with questions about navigation, airfield lighting, Air Law etc, very similar to that for the Highway Code.) The standards varied. Some achieved solo flight in 9, 10 or 11 hours, one girl did it in 7½ hours, and over 13 hours and the applicant was failed. One young man made a name for himself on his first solo. Five times he attempted a landing on his first solo, opening his throttle and making straight for the control tower each time. Five times the control staff rushed down the stairs from their position on the roof of the terminal building. The would-be pilot made it on his sixth attempt, but was not asked to come again.'

At least this tyro pilot managed to land himself, not so with another trainee as is remembered by fellow CAG member, Bill Stone:

'One of the pilots just couldn't seem to land his aircraft while on his first solo flight, and after several attempts, two of the instructors took off in the other Hornet Moths and formatted on his wing tips to guide him down safely.

A line-up of Thanet Aero Club aircraft in August 1939. Nearest the camera is Piper J-4A Cub Coupe G-AFVM; next Tiger Moth G-AFSR and last in line two DH.87B Hornet Moths G-AFDY and G-AFEE. (Photo via R. Riding)

The terminal building at Ramsgate Airport, which housed offices, a restaurant, lounge, bar and clubroom of Thanet Aero Club. On the roof is the air traffic control cabin and wireless room. (Photo via Mr R. Riding)

'Once we had gone solo and had one or two hours solo flying to our credit, one stunt was to fly out to Deal and then back to Ramsgate at 'nil' feet, right into the harbour entrance and pull up over the Eastern Arm. The Lieutenant Commander, who was the Harbour Master, wrote to Squadron Leader Maslin to say "If your fledglings persist in making my harbour a playground, I will have to charge them harbour dues." As we had a dining-in night once a month, the Harbour Master was invited to attend one of these, and after a good meal and hospitality, taken up in one of the club's aircraft and treated to a low-level "beat-up" of the harbour himself."

By December 1938 there were some 40 CAG members under training, and despite the inclement weather during the next three months, an average of 30 hours were flown by club members and several pilots gained their 'A' licences or went solo. In February 1939 one of the founder members of the club, Mr Albert Bachelor of 'Bleak House', Broadstairs, donated four of his aircraft to the club. The prototype De Havilland DH90 Dragonfly G-ADNA, the Cievra C-30A autogiro G-ACWM and his Miles Whitney Straight G-AFBV being added to the Thanet Aero Club's fleet. Other machines which were used by the club were two side-by-side seat trainers, Tipsy S.2 G-AEYG and the Czech-designed Hillson-Praga G-AEYL and De Havilland Tiger Moth G-AFSR, the latter two machines being part of the Straight Organisation fleet allocated to their various aerodromes.

The first dinner and dance for the Civil Air Guard members was held at the end of April 1939, when it was stated that there had been 344 applications for membership, of whom 121 had been enrolled, and of that number 29 had taken their 'A' licence test and a further 21 had made their first solo flights. Of the newly qualified pilots, there was one girl, Miss Muriel Burke of Margate, and the guest speaker, Group Captain W.V. Strugnell, M.C., Officer Commanding RAF Manston, made a mention of this in his after dinner speech:

'The Civil Air Guard is open to both sexes, and I have been told that some of the lady members are very good indeed, although they don't know what they will be up against in time of trouble.

'There are three things which all members must have — keenness, physical fitness and discipline. You need keenness, because in time of strife there will be all sorts of unpleasant jobs for the Civil Air Guard to do, like the ferrying of decrepit old aeroplanes that have been shot about, and to which older pilots have said "No, No!".'

From this remark it would appear that the role of the Civil Air Guard was seen at the time as doing the same sort of work as the Air Transport Auxiliary was to undertake during World War Two, the delivery of new aircraft from factory to airfield and the collection of damaged aircraft for repair.

During the week ending 8th May 1939, some twenty-five members of the CAG units attached to Straight Organisation aerodromes had taken part in the Margate National Service Parade, together with ARP, Auxiliary Fire Service, Red Cross and other volunteer organisations. Another parade was held at Broadstairs in June, one of those attending was John Rootes:

'When I gained my 'A' licence, I was made Unit Commander of the local Cliftonville Section, which didn't involve very much, only that I was entitled to wear a thin yellow stripe on my uniform epaulettes. Another parade was held at Ramsgate Airport on 24th June when we were inspected by the local MP, Captain Harold H. Balfour, and as we marched past I spotted my sister with her camera taking a photo·— I couldn't resist the temptation to flash a quick smile at her as we passed.'

Activity continued apace during the summer of 1939, both at the Thanet Aero Club and at the Holiday Flying Centre, which was an aviation holiday camp at the airport. Visitors could book in for a fortnight's holiday and receive training as part of the Civil Air Guard while their families enjoyed the opportunity of making joy-rides in the airport's aircraft or relaxing on local sands. By the end of June 1939 there were some 120 bookings made for the Holiday Flying Centre, twenty of the visitors were undertaking CAG training. In the week ending 17th July some 206 hours were recorded in the air by club members, and despite inclement weather on some days during the rest of July and August, over 180 hours were achieved during the week ending 17th August and also during the final week of the month.

On the outbreak of war, the members of the Civil Air Guard were ready to play their part in helping the RAF, but were doomed to disappointment, Peter Beechey recounts his experience:

'When the war came we all received our "Call-Up" notices to go and do our duty, but I got the very definite feeling that the RAF didn't want anything to do with us at all. They looked on us as freaks, and they wanted to train people from scratch rather than have semi-trained pilots. There were people like myself, who had 26½ hours flying, had just got my 'A' licence and a few hours solo. I went forward to volunteer for flying duties, but they just didn't want me, and I think there were a lot of other people who were disillusioned like myself.'

John Rootes also had a similar experience:

'War came, and six eager young men, clutching their pilot's 'A' licences, presented themselves at the Air Ministry. They told us "Sorry chaps, but we have enough pilots. However, in view of your training we will accept you as air gunners!" So they became — and wondered what it was all about. Some twelve months later, those of the six who were still alive were asked to re-muster as pilots!'

Acknowledgements: Mr P. Beechey; Mr J. Rootes; Mr W. Stone; Mr J.T. Huddlestone; 'Flight' magazine.

## Chapter 6

# THE OBSERVER CORPS
# Its Formative Years in Kent

### By A.J. Moor

If you ever pass through the charming town of Cranbrook and decide to take a stroll along the High Street, you may notice a plaque on the front of the former Gateway Stores which during the early 1920s was a Post Office. On closer inspection the following dedication reads:

'The first
Royal Observer Corps
Operations Room
was located in this building
in 1925.

THIS PLAQUE WAS ERECTED TO COMMEMORATE
THE 50TH ANNIVERSARY OF THE CORPS
BY SERVING AND FORMER MEMBERS
OF THE ROYAL OBSERVER CORPS

MCMLXXVI'

The story of the Royal Observer Corps begins during the First World War with an air raid on East London by the airship LZ38 on the night of 31st May 1915, which brought home the need for well-organised air defences. At that time anti-aircraft positions amounted to twelve, backed up by ten isolated fighter units. As yet no official body had been formed to report enemy aircraft sightings. This responsibility had been given to the Army, the local constabulary, and railway stations. Details were relayed by telephone to the Kent Constabulary who contacted the 'Intelligence London Advise Headquarters 2nd Army' at Tunbridge Wells or the Chief Constable at Maidstone. As a result the information was usually received too late.

In June 1917 German Gotha and Staaken Giants, both of which were large biplane bombers, replaced earlier raids of the Zeppelin airships. A Government inquiry followed resulting in the combining of all ground and air defences under the leadership of General E.B. Ashmore, who had been in command of the 29th Artillery Division at Ypres. On July 31st 1917 Ashmore was appointed to command the newly-formed London Air Defence Area (LADA). Within ten days

This group of gentlemen formed the Pluckley ROC post F3 during the war. Note the vicar, top row, who no doubt was exceptional at spotting 'heavenly bodies'. Left to right: back row: Rev. Bowen, W. Jennings, A. Black, J. Blackman, P. Luckhurst, R. Sells; second row: A. Luckhurst, F.V. Weeks, Oldham, A.G. Homewood, G. Finn; bottom row: H. Brissenden, N. Buss, R. Small, A. Leonard.                    (A.G. Homewood)

Situated at West Hythe this 30 foot diameter 'bowl mirror' formed part of two lines of similar sound detectors running parallel to the Kent coast in the 1920s. These concrete discs would have helped to protect England from aerial attack during 1939-45 had it not been for the advent of radar and the birth of the Observer Corps.           (A.J. Moor)

he had established a defence line 20 miles east of London which was patrolled by fighters.

By the summer of 1918 Ashmore had created a workable system. Observers on the coast, after hearing an aircraft, reported the horizontal bearing and vertical angle to a sub-control. Having plotted the information the duty officer phoned the LADA duty officer in London. It was then decided whether this was in fact a hostile aircraft. If other reports confirmed this and there was evidence to suggest a raid was 'on' the LADA duty officer ordered 'Readiness'. An operator rang the sub-controls while Signals men warned the authorities. Progress of an enemy aircraft could be plotted on a map, and AA guns, searchlights and fighters swung into action.

The Armistice came in November 1918, the year Ashmore's system was established. He drew up a proposal for peacetime air defence, on 22nd November 1918, retaining the command structure he had created. In 1920 he was given the post of Commander, Air Defence Brigade.

Responsibility for Air Defence was given to the War Office in 1922. A committee was formed in 1924 headed by Major General C.F. Romer, to investigate warning and communications systems, as a result of the cabinet plans to expand the RAF to 52 squadrons. One proposal was for an observation system with posts which gave details of sightings to observer units who in turn informed the Fighter Area HQ. Some of these observer units would be linked direct to fighter sectors. In January 1924 the Air Raid Precautions sub-committee was appointed, and became linked with the observation system. It was felt by the Romer Committee that 'the civilian population will be so vitally affected by air attacks that the responsibility of observation and warning cannot be considered exclusively military'. Ashmore was on the Romer Committee and organised an exercise to determine the following:

A) The best distance apart to put the posts.
B) The number of posts that could work to one observation centre.
C) The best method of passing the 'Readiness' signal to the posts and centres.
D) The best method of reporting.
E) The best locating apparatus if required.

The locations for this experiment were to be Romney Marsh and Tonbridge. For this purpose special constables and civilians were recruited. In a letter to the Chief Constable of Kent, Major H.E. Chapman, Ashmore asked if he would organise a small group of observation posts and an operations room. This exercise was termed 'Air Defence Observation in the Weald of Kent, 1924'. Constables were to man posts organised into groups of three for communications. They were: Sutton Valence, Goudhurst, Marden, Cranbrook, Bethersden, Ham Street, Biddenden, Hawkhurst and Tenterden.

Cranbrook Post Office became the operations room while Ashmore and his officers visited the posts. Each post had a basic wooden instrument mounted on a tripod. A head and breast set was used to communicate via a telephone box

THE CORPS IS CALLED OUT

HISTORY OF THE R·O·C.
24ᵗʰ AUGUST 1939

by D. Cleverley

This cartoon depicting the Observer Corps call-out on 24th August 1939 typifies the spirit of the volunteer Observer. They came from all walks of life and formed the backbone of the Corps.

(ROC Journal)

Sopwich Snipes of 32 Squadron seen here at Lympne airfield during 1924. In one of these aircraft F/O D.M. Fleming conducted the exercise which was to determine the future of the Observer Corps. The aircraft here carry the squadron's new blue and white marking from nose to tail. The roundels being red and blue only.

(J.D.R. Rawlings)

connec___ to a telegraph pole. The instrument, which was similar to a panto-graph, s___d on end with its pivot through a map table. There were two pins on the long a__ of the pantograph which were used for sighting the aircraft. This instrumen___ ___as the forerunner of the 'Post Instrument' introduced in 1935 and used by t__ Corps for 25 years. To plot an aircraft an upright rod traversed across the ___ap. When the height (measured in feet) coincided with the lower arm of th__ ___antograph the square indicated gave the aircraft's location. Maps used had__ grid of 3 mile squares each grid being labelled HW, NW etc. This enabled t__ ___ observer to determine the aircraft's position. To the grid reading the comp___s direction was added.

Exercises took place on 12th, 15th, and 19th August and 9th September, night tests being held on 2nd and 5th September. Flying Officer D.M. Fleming of 32 Squadron took off in his Sopwith Snipe on the afternoon of 12th August, flying from Kenley to Hawkinge. He flew along the Downs approaching from the north. Sutton Valence reported the aircraft at 6 p.m. to Cranbrook, as being in grid reference HS. It became clear that this method was workable as for the next hour all posts reported sighting Fleming's Snipe.

With the success of the 1924 experiments Ashmore turned his attention to expansion. He decided to organise temporary controls or operations rooms in both Kent and Sussex. Chief constables were asked to organise 44 posts in two groups, the group headquarters being located at Maidstone and Horsham. Using a grid of between eight and ten miles locations were chosen and the GPO asked to provide telephone lines to each. These control centres were at post offices. Mr J.H. Day was appointed superintendent for Maidstone. Special constables were then sworn in and asked not to reveal to anyone what they had been recruited for. The following towns and villages were selected for posts forming No.1 Group, Maidstone:

| | | |
|---|---|---|
| A1 Minster | D1 Eastchurch | H1 Catsfield |
| A2 Ash | D2 Queenborough | H2 Robertsbridge |
| A3 Chislet | D3 Sittingbourne | H3 Beckley |
| B1 Whitstable | F1 Hamstreet | E1 Faversham |
| B2 Canterbury | F2 Bethersden | E2 Sheldwich Lees |
| B3 Wye | F3 Little Chart | E3 Lenham |
| C1 Eythorne | G1 Cranbrook | J1 Horsmonden |
| C2 Barham | G2 Headcorn | J2 Ticehurst |
| C3 Lyminge | G3 Tenterden | J3 Frant |

By late June 1925 all posts had been supplied with plotting and telephone equipment. Exercises took place using three RAF squadrons flying by day and night to enable the plotters to gain experience. It was recommended that further groups be formed in Hampshire and Essex, thus completing the net-work. With the approval of the Committee of Imperial Defence in October 1925 the Observer Corps was established. Certificates were issued to some 300 Observers who had proved themselves in both aircraft recognition and plotting

In 1975 Mrs E. Ashmore, widow of Major General E.B. Ashmore, CB, CMG, MVO, unveiled the plaque, pictured above. This can still be seen today on the wall of the vacant Gateways store, once a post office, in Cranbrook High Street. (A.J. Moor)

procedures. The late H.E. Ward, whilst Headmaster of a school in Headcorn, had a meeting with General Ashmore. As a result Mr Ward became Head Observer of the Headcorn post and was certified No.122 on the official list of qualified corps members.

After 1925 six exercises were conducted each year in June and July from 6 until 7 p.m. They were for communication and calibration. During 1927 Major General Ashmore, Wing Commander Holt, and Mr C. de Parry, H.M. Inspector of Constabulary, visited both Maidstone and Lenham, and were impressed by the enthusiasm shown and progress being made at the posts.

Towards the end of 1928 the War Office relinquished its control of the Corps to the RAF. The new Commandant was Air Commodore E.A.D. Masterman. By this time there were four Groups — No.1 Maidstone, No.2 Horsham, No.3 Winchester and No.18 Colchester.

In 1933 public attention in Kent was drawn to the Corps when Mr J.H. Day, Maidstone's Superintendent, was awarded the MBE for his services to the Corps. That same year the RAF introduced a new map grid, on a 20 inch diameter chart.

Mr H.E. Ward, mentioned earlier, recalled that he later left the Headcorn post in 1936 and was transferred to the Maidstone centre. He was stationed at the Corn Exchange, but later at Maidstone Post Office. To get to the plotting room he had to climb an outside staircase. Plotting was done using coloured counters on a large table map of Kent.

Up until 1939 annual exercises took place in Kent spotting and recording heights of aircraft. The reports were relayed to the Maidstone centre. Observers were not issued with uniform. However they were given two waterproof capes because as yet the outlying posts had no shelters. A button badge had also been issued to each and every Observer.

An ex-member of the original Pluckley post, Mr A.G. Homewood, remembers they met each week in a local field, which was owned at the time by Mr Headley the grocer. To report their sightings they would connect a portable telephone to a terminal box on a telegraph pole which had been wired for the purpose by the GPO. Mr Homewood was introduced to the Corps by his father who had been a special constable. He later became an Observer Instructor, and stayed with the Corps until just after the war.

For some time the Army had been trying to establish long-range detection which would give early warning to the Observer Corps of incoming aircraft. They had constructed large concrete dishes which ranged from 15ft to 200ft in diameter. These dishes could detect sound up to 21 miles distant but the idea was dropped after many experiments, the main failing of the system being that it was impossible to detect the number of aircraft approaching.

With the adoption of radar the Observer Corps expanded. As radar was shrouded in secrecy during the late thirties only the Commandant knew something of its secrets. The Observer was not so well-informed, and morale suffered. An officer who inspected the Observer post at Wye remarked in his report that he had trouble in convincing the post crew that the Corps was a 'seriously considered organisation'.

In July 1936 Observer posts at Faversham, Whitstable, Sheerness, Deal, Lenham and Canterbury were introduced to another innovation, that of sound amplifiers. The assistance of local wireless agents was employed to explain the system to the post Observers. The amplifier was used to extend audible range. This instrument was in fact turned down in October 1936. In 1937 the Air Ministry received a proposal from Captain G.K. Chambers who lived at Sitting-bourne. The design was for an instrument, not unlike a megaphone, which measured 1' 6" long, containing a baffle. The small diameter end was held to the air by a copper handle. After extensive tests the Commandant rejected the invention as it did not improve the range.

With the German escalation of munitions a Home Defence Sub-Committee headed by Sir Hugh Dowding in 1937 called for 45 fighter squadrons, 1,200 anti-aircraft guns, 5,000 searchlights, radar, radio and further expansion of the Observer Corps. By the time of the Munich Crisis in 1938 it was agreed that national coverage by the Corps was essential. The Air Raid Warden Service had already been formed. Apart from No.1 Maidstone Group, No.19 Bromley Group had been formed officially in 1937. Bromley Group would give cover to the north, east and south.

Exercises were organised to improve communications and unite the RAF with its new partner. On 5th/7th August 1938 one such Home Defence exercise took place. There were already five radar stations (RDF) in existence, the ones at Great Bromley and Dover being the most recent. It became apparent that there were problems in communications caused by the multitude of sightings. This led to further recruitment and four watches created to train Observers throughout the network.

No.1 Group had already completed eight days and nights on watch. Dowding had in fact, in secrecy, put the Observer Corps on a wartime basis on 24th August.

On 3rd September 1939 the air raid sirens sounded prematurely when a French aircraft failed to file its flight plan. The aircraft was considered hostile, it had been located by radar. It flew over the domain of No.1 Group Maidstone and No.19 Group Bromley. No one was able to identify the intruder so it was reported as a 'plane'!

That same day Neville Chamberlain solemnly informed the nation that it was at war with Nazi Germany. For the next five and a half years all Observer posts in Kent would be permanently manned.

Footnote: In April 1941 in reply to questions concerning the work of the Observer Corps, Sir Archibald Sinclair informed the House of Commons that His Majesty the King had been graciously pleased to approve that the Corps should thenceforth be known by the style and description of 'The Royal Observer Corps'.

Acknowledgements to Mr D. Wood ('Attack Warning Red'); Mr A.G. Homewood; Mr D. Gower; ROC Journal.

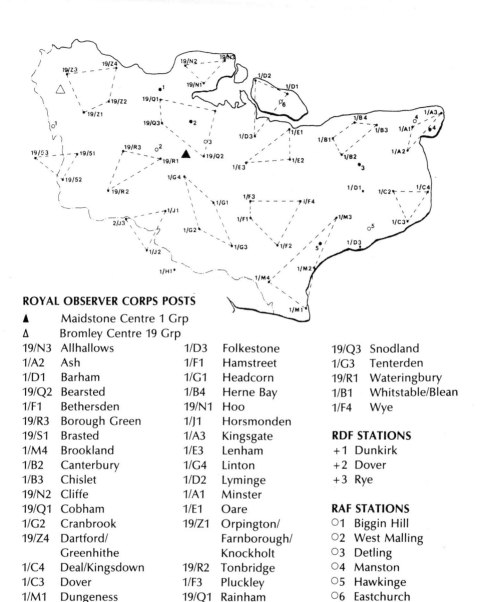

## ROYAL OBSERVER CORPS POSTS

▲     Maidstone Centre 1 Grp
△     Bromley Centre 19 Grp

| | | | | | | |
|---|---|---|---|---|---|---|
| 19/N3 | Allhallows | 1/D3 | Folkestone | 19/Q3 | Snodland |
| 1/A2 | Ash | 1/F1 | Hamstreet | 1/G3 | Tenterden |
| 1/D1 | Barham | 1/G1 | Headcorn | 19/R1 | Wateringbury |
| 19/Q2 | Bearsted | 1/B4 | Herne Bay | 1/B1 | Whitstable/Blean |
| 1/F1 | Bethersden | 19/N1 | Hoo | 1/F4 | Wye |
| 19/R3 | Borough Green | 1/J1 | Horsmonden | | |
| 19/S1 | Brasted | 1/A3 | Kingsgate | **RDF STATIONS** | |
| 1/M4 | Brookland | 1/E3 | Lenham | +1 | Dunkirk |
| 1/B2 | Canterbury | 1/G4 | Linton | +2 | Dover |
| 1/B3 | Chislet | 1/D2 | Lyminge | +3 | Rye |
| 19/N2 | Cliffe | 1/A1 | Minster | | |
| 19/Q1 | Cobham | 1/E1 | Oare | **RAF STATIONS** | |
| 1/G2 | Cranbrook | 19/Z1 | Orpington/ | ○1 | Biggin Hill |
| 19/Z4 | Dartford/ | | Farnborough/ | ○2 | West Malling |
| | Greenhithe | | Knockholt | ○3 | Detling |
| 1/C4 | Deal/Kingsdown | 19/R2 | Tonbridge | ○4 | Manston |
| 1/C3 | Dover | 1/F3 | Pluckley | ○5 | Hawkinge |
| 1/M1 | Dungeness | 19/Q1 | Rainham | ○6 | Eastchurch |
| 1/M2 | Dymchurch | 1/H1 | Seddlescombe/ | | |
| 19/T1 | Eastchurch | | E. Sussex | **CIVIL AERODROMES** | |
| 19/S2 | Edenbridge | 19/T2 | Sheerness | ●1 | Gravesend |
| 19/Z3 | Eltham | 1/E2 | Sheldwich Leas | ●2 | Rochester |
| 1/C1 | Eythorn | 19/T3 | Sittingbourne/ | ●3 | Bekesbourne |
| 19/Z2 | Farningham | | Rodmersham | ●4 | Ramsgate |
| | | | Green | ●5 | Lympne |

The 468th (Cinque Ports) Company RE, at camp at Fort Langdon, Dover, in May 1937, checking lorries and equipment. L/Corp R.S. Body, 5th from left, sitting on a pile of boxes.
(Photo via Mr R.S. Body)

A Mark 9 mobile sound locator outside the Drill Hall, with Sergeant Metcalfe seated and civilian maintenance man, Mr Lewis, standing at the front.        (Photo via R.S. Body)

Chapter 7

# EAST KENT'S
# SEARCHLIGHT VOLUNTEERS
## The 468th (Cinque Ports)
## Searchlight Company RE, 1938 – 39

### By David G. Collyer

In 1836 – 37 two troops of East Kent Horse Yeomanry were disbanded and it was exactly 100 years later that another Territorial Army unit was established when the country was again fearful of a threat from the Continent. In 1936 Mr J.C. Allnat of St Mary's Bay Holiday Camp arranged to hold a number of local meetings to assess public support, and as a result the Kent Territorial Army and Air Force Association was approached with the idea of the formation of a local TA unit.

Authority was given for a detachment of the Dover-based, searchlight-equipped, Cinque Ports (Fortress) Company Royal Engineers to be formed in Romney Marsh. Early in October 1936 a Royal Engineer Sergeant, J.W. Pike, was posted to St Mary's Bay as Permanent Staff Instructor (PSI), the Holiday Camp providing rent free the necessary buildings, with Lieutenant J.C. Allnat in charge. It was proposed that the Romney Marsh unit should have officers and NCOs on its own and that if the numbers reached 100, then a Headquarters Drill Hall would be built. By the end of May 1937, the 100 number had been reached, and the unit went to camp at Fort Langdon (near Dover) — 9 brand new Tilling Stevens petrol electric lorries were provided, complete with searchlights and ancillary equipment. The power for the searchlights was supplied by a unique arrangement utilising the TSM petrol engine of the lorry. This could either supply power via a generator for the searchlight, or for the electric motor which propelled the vehicle without any gears.

Nine Searchlight Detachments of ten men went out most evenings to train and practise, and on some nights a civilian aircraft from Lympne aerodrome was provided as a target. Much was learned and no mishaps occurred. In 1937 land for the Drill Hall was purchased and the new building commenced, and by 1938 it was in use by the 468th (Cinque Ports) Searchlight Company, Royal Engineers, as the company was now known.

On 26th September 1938, as a result of Hitler's aggressive activities, all British Home Defence Anti-Aircraft Forces were mobilised, and as a result four parties of 34 men under a sergeant were sent to airfields to defend them against low

A 90 cms searchlight in a permanent installation manned by the Searchlight Controller and the No.5 who looked after the arc lamp. (Photo via Imperial War Museum No.H1291)

flying aircraft. Because of equipment deficiencies the Company could only man four searchlights instead of the usual 24, and they had only had two lectures on the six Lewis guns with which each party was equipped.

One of those who was 'mobilised' was Mr R.S. 'Dick' Body of Hope Farm at Snargate:

'By September 1938 I had been made acting Sergeant as I had attended a course for potential Senior NCOs at the School of Aerial Defence at Biggin Hill in February, for both gunners and searchlight detachment commanders. On Monday 26th September a local policeman called on me and told me to report to the Drill Hall as all air defence units that could be were being mobilised without the need of a Royal Proclamation.

'When I got to the Drill Hall about 5.30 p.m. we were split into two parties, one for Eastchurch aerodrome and one for Manston. I was in the party sent to Eastchurch with 34 men and six Lewis guns, with which we were to defend the aerodrome, plus two searchlight detachments. We arrived at Eastchurch about midnight and were not expected, but the Station Warrant Officer organised a NAAFI meal, and then we bedded down on coconut mats in the gymnasium.

'First thing on Tuesday morning we all had a medical inspection, and I was isolated until the MO found out what sheep tick bites were, as I had several nasty looking ones around the groin. The party moved into one of the RAF Boy Apprentices' huts, and later, having drawn picks, shovels and sandbags, marched past the Station HQ to an earth dump to start filling sandbags. Very soon an order came through from the Station HQ that all men must wear their caps at all times. However, a third of the party had only recently joined and had no uniforms or caps, only brown overalls.

'We were placed under a Squadron Leader Stevens, and more directly a civilian instructor, an ex-Tank Corps Captain, and we all got on very well together. The sites for the six Lewis gun posts around the airfield perimeter were selected for us and everybody got busy filling sandbags, carting them and building the gun pits. Lessons were soon learned about beating down each layer of bags tight otherwise the walls collapsed.

'On Wednesday Sergeant Miller of the Dover part of the Company arrived with his 34 men from Gravesend Aerodrome, having been told that they were not wanted there as the RAF had not taken over the civilian aerodrome. He and I did not see alike; perhaps rightly he felt that we should come under his orders and parade under him. My party did not parade each morning but went straight to our sandbag filling duties. I had a word with our civilian instructor, who in turn consulted the Squadron Leader and I got permission to carry on as before — Sergeant Miller was not very happy.

'Most of Thursday was spent trying to degrease the guns, which had probably been put on in 1918 or soon afterwards and on Friday the RAF gave us instruction on our guns and fixed up mountings for them.

'Chamberlain and Hitler having met at Munich on Thursday, and having put something on paper, the crisis was apparently removed, and as a result on Saturday 1st October a message came through that all those not required could go home on indefinite leave. The RAF produced passes and warrants and with Lance Corporal Beeching volunteering to stay behind to take charge of the guns, all departed homewards.'

During 1939 recruiting and training continued and the Territorial Forces were greatly enlarged, and all Air Defence Forces had to undergo four weeks' training on actual searchlight sites. By now the Romney Marsh Company had reached a strength of 200 men and normal fortnight annual camp was cancelled, a quarter of each company going in turn, i.e. one section doing four months training on war sites. The Romney Marsh Company was allocated sites in Essex, the two Dover sections going first, followed by one Romney Marsh section, and this one was on site at General Mobilisation on Monday 24th August 1939. 'Dick' Body was working on the farm as usual:

'On this afternoon I was bindering wheat at Pinkney Bush, and when a policeman arrived, he was not unexpected. I was now a full sergeant — Section Sergeant to No.4 Section. When we had all been medically inspected by Dr Purser, who just asked us "How are you?", we all passed and drew various

Section HQ for No.4 Section at Upton Wood, Shepherdswell in September 1939.
(Photo via R.S. Body)

stores and two days' rations. With our TSM lorries, plus two lorries hired from
Carey Brothers, we proceeded to the Lydden Mobilisation Store, where the rest
of our searchlights and equipment were waiting. The Army had sent a number
of towing trucks to get the Lister trailer diesel generators and the searchlights to
the various sites. Unfortunately the Army trucks were not big enough to take the
searchlights, so the TSMs had to go with all the lights to the various sites. My
section was lucky, their sites were all within a six-mile radius of the Mobilisation
Store and No.4 Section got its equipment away that night. We arrived at the
Section HQ at Upton Wood, Shepherdswell about 3.30 a.m. — not a movement
anywhere, everybody and everything laying everywhere, all shining in the head-
lights with a heavy dew covering all.'

The 24 searchlights were spread all over East Kent — east of a line from
Cheriton, Littlebourne and Herne Bay — from Folkestone, Swingfield and
Selstead via Shepherdswell, Aylesham and St Radigund's, Littlebourne, Bishops-
bourne, Wingham, Kingsdown, Sandwich Golf Links to Acol and Chislet
Colliery. Within 24 hours all the searchlights were operational. Each section had
ten men with an NCO in charge, who was known as No.1; while Nos 2 and 3
were 'spotters' who reclined in revolving chairs and searched the sky using
binoculars. The SLC (Searchlight Controller) was No.4 and was directed by
either Nos 2 and 3, or by No.6, another NCO, who was in charge of the sound
locator and connected by a telephone line with the SLC and directed him where
to aim the beam. The sound locator consisted of two pairs of trumpet-shaped
horns mounted on a movable frame which could follow the sound of an aircraft
either in elevation or in azimuth (sideways) and was manned by Nos 7 and 8, the
'listeners' who had stethoscope earpieces connected to the trumpets. The
generator was sited some 300 yards away so as not to interfere with the
'listeners' and was manned by No.9. Of the remaining section members, No.5

was in charge of the searchlight arc lamp while No.10 was the section cook. 'Dick' Body describes how the direction sytem worked':

'We tried to site our 'spotters' about 25 yards from the 'light' and the only directions given to the SLC by the 'spotters' or the No.6 were "Left . . . Right" or "Up . . . Down and Stop" — followed by "On Target", when the SLC automatically continued to keep the target in the beam. The "Up", "Down", "Left" or "Right" being given fast or in a drawl, for the beam to be moved quickly or slowly. On Tuesday 25th August the tents were erected and a telephone line installed to the Company HQ at Wingham, and we set about building the Section HQ and making ourselves as comfortable as possible. The walls were of sandbags while the corrugated iron roof and door were scrounged by Staff Sergeant Willicott from Lydd Camp; the windows at each end were old car doors I scrounged from Lines Brothers, car breakers of Wooton, and these could even be raised and lowered.

'As Section Sergeant, after the first two days I had to draw rations from the Company HQ and distribute them to the sites at Selstead (Snodehill Farm), Folkestone (Cricket Ground), Swingfield (Evenden Farm), St Radigund's (Abbey Farm) and Aylesham — weren't the kids a nuisance there! I got on very well with the Company Quarter Master Sergeant Prescott at the ration store, and again I seemed to get preferential treatment, but I never saw so many wasps as there were at the ration store.

'We were lucky in our section headquarters, as we had one of the Holiday Camp cooks and soon after mobilisation I went to Messrs Arter Brothers, Agricultural Engineers of Barham and scrounged 12 oil drums to build field ovens, and some cast iron pipes for chimneys. I also scrounged some straw from where a threshing machine was working for the palliases and a good supply of broken pit props at Snowdown Colliery which we could use as fuel.'

After the hurried deployment, the Army started to catch up with the necessary form filling, and this provided something of a problem for Sergeant Body:

'When we were leaving Lydden, the driver of the last lorry told me that he needed some petrol, so I sent him to the fuel store. The man in charge said, "Well, all this is yours!", and we had all the Company paraffin, grease, lubricating oil and most of the petrol. Nothing signed for, plus the company stores.

'A Lance Corporal Layton of Dover was put in charge of fuel and he was soon after me to sign for what we had had from Lydden. I only offered to sign for what we had had — if he told me the amount. In the end somebody decided that each section should sign for a quarter — I was quite happy with this.'

By Sunday 3rd September 1939, all those who were near a wireless at 11 o'clock will never forget Chamberlain's broadcast that 'Britain is at war'. This was followed by the air raid sirens sounding all over Britain, but in the fields of East Kent the searchlight volunteers were ready and waiting.

Acknowledgements to Mr R.S. Body who provided the majority of this article from his own personal reminiscences and that of the 468th (Cinque Ports) Searchlight Company Royal Engineers, also the photographs.

Chapter 8

# THE ORDER OF BATTLE OF THE RAF IN KENT, 1938–39

## By Geoff Baxter

It might be said that success at arms involves three main factors:
(1)  The arms used.
(2)  The courage and skill of the users.
(3)  The quality of the leaders.

With the passage of time the development of arms has assumed greater importance. This was well illustrated by the 1939–45 war and the years immediately preceding it.

In 1938 the Luftwaffe had reached a high point with its units equipped with Me109s, He111s and Ju88s. The Regia Aeronautica had peaked earlier and was into a period of comparative decline. The Armée de l'Air of France, was still the largest European Air Force but composed largely of obsolete aircraft, a situation exacerbated by the political chaos which blocked any hope of modernisation.

In Britain the RAF was just completing a move from the biplane era, but with the established radar chain, which was still somewhat erratic, was not too badly placed.

This then was the state of the future combatants against which the Order of Battle of the RAF in Kent must be viewed.

Bomber Command was not present in the area except for units under training.

Fighter Command's function was defence of the area, especially the London and Thames Estuary areas. In this respect it should be remembered that an immediate bombing attack was anticipated after the declaration of war.

Coastal Command unit's function was seen as assisting the Navy to control the Channel and southern North Sea.

As in the rest of the United Kingdom, preparations in Kent had been stimulated by the nation-wide defence exercise of August 1939.

# ORDER OF BATTLE OF THE ROYAL AIR FORCE IN KENT 1938–39

## AIR MINISTRY

| Fighter Command | Army Co-op | Coastal | Flying Training | Bomber |
|---|---|---|---|---|
| 11 Group | | 16 Group | 26 Group | |
| 3 Squadron | 2 Squadron | 22 Squadron | 20 E & R FS | 21 Squadron |
| 25 | | 48 | 23 E & R FS | (To 2 Group) |
| 32 | | 500 | | |
| 79 | | | | |
| 235 | | **Fleet Air Arm** | | |
| 253 | | HMS *Daedalus II* | | |
| | | 816 Squadron | | |
| | | 818 | | |

E & R FS = Elementary and Reserve Flying School

## NOTES ON THE ORDER OF BATTLE

### 2 Squadron
This unit flying Hector Is on Army Co-operation duties was posted from Manston to Hawkinge in 1935. After converting to Lysander Is in September 1939 they finally left Hawkinge on 6th September 1939 to join the Air Component of the BEF and were based at Abbeville-Drucat airfield. They eventually returned to Kent after the fall of France.

### 3 Squadron
Flew Gladiator Is before converting to Hurricanes and moving from Kenley to Biggin Hill on 2nd May 1939, staying there for four months. After a few days flying from Croydon and a similar period at Manston during September 1939, they returned to Croydon on posting leaving a detachment at Hawkinge from 17.12.39 to 10.2.40 when the whole squadron flew out to Merville, France. They were to continue in the fighter role throughout the war and to re-appear in Kent in both 1943 and 1944.

### 21 Squadron
This light bomber squadron was based at Lympne until 15th August 1938, flying Hinds. Thereafter they moved to Eastchurch and converted to Blenheim Is. They were posted to their war station, Watton, early in March 1939, but were to be found again in Kent shortly before D-Day flying from Manston and Gravesend.

### 22 Squadron
Although this unit was stationed at Thorney Island flying Wildebeests, from the beginning of 1938 it had detachments at other airfields in the SE including one at Detling. These were for anti-submarine duties in the Channel. During the

latter part of 1939 they began to convert to Beauforts, but it is not known if any of these reached Detling.

## 25 Squadron

Flew Demons (2-seater fighters) from Hawkinge mid-1938 before converting to Gladiators until December 1938 when Blenheim Is began to arrive.

## 32 Squadron

With Squadron Leader K. Pyne in command, 32 Squadron were involved in a London defence role with Gauntlet IIs at Biggin Hill. In 1939 they converted to Hurricane Is and left for Gravesend on 3rd March 1940.

## 34 Squadron

Lympne was the base for this squadron during the first half of 1938, flying Hinds in the light bomber role. On 11th July 1938 they moved to Upper Heyford, where they converted to Blenheim Is.

## 48 Squadron

Spent most of the war flying on coastal duties, but transferred to Transport Command on Dakotas early in 1944.

At Manston throughout the period 16.12.35 – 1.9.38, they operated Anson Is under Wing Commander J.L. Findlay, mostly on training duties for No.16 Group. Their next move was to Eastchurch, leaving a detachment at Manston. Immediately before the outbreak of war they were transferred to Thorney Island, but even then left a detachment at Detling. Eventually they moved from the South-East in August 1939 on posting to Hooton Park to carry out reconnaissance over the Irish Sea and Western Approaches.

## 79 Squadron

Biggin Hill was also the base for this unit, flying Gauntlet IIs until December 1938 and commanded by Squadron Leader N.A. Prichett. In November 1939 they moved to Manston to fly defensive patrols for four months, having converted to Hurricane Is a year earlier.

## 235 Squadron

Re-formed on 30th November 1939 at Manston. They were intended to become a fighter squadron, but it was thought at the time that there might be a sudden urgent need for fighters for the front line squadrons. As an interim solution they received Fairey Battles to enable pilots to become familiar with single engined monoplane flying. The aircraft being received in December, before much experience was gained they were transferred to Coastal Command in February 1940 and posted to North Coates.

## 253 Squadron

The formation of this unit started on the same day as 235 Squadron and also at Manston. With the similarity of the numbers it seems that the opportunity for confusion was high. The intention was to equip them with Blenheim Is but aircraft of this type were not available and eventually in February 1940 it received Hurricane Is.

**500 Squadron** (County of Kent)

Formed at Manston as early as March 1931 as a Special Reserve Squadron with part regular and part reserve personnel. By 1937 it was a light bomber unit equipped with Hawker Harts, but a year earlier the Air Ministry had decided that its nature should change from a reserve to an auxiliary squadron.

On 7th November 1938 it transferred to Coastal Command and began to re-equip with Anson Is, moving to Detling in September 1938, with Squadron Leader L. Hohler as CO.

Apart from a fortnight at Warmwell in Dorset, 500 stayed at Detling until May 1941, flying patrols and convoy escorts over the Channel and North Sea.

It continued this type of operation from the UK and in the Mediterranean until 1944, and only returned to Kent as a R.Aux.A.F. squadron based at West Malling in 1946.

**Fleet Air Arm**

**HMS *Daedalus II*** six Skuas and 3 Rocs from HMS *Ark Royal* formed this training unit, having first been named HMS *Buzzard* at Lympne. This brief naval episode appears to have lasted from July to September 1939 when the aircraft were re-embarked on the *Ark*.

Another brief naval encounter took place at Manston in the autumn of 1939 when 816 and 818 (FAA) Squadrons formed.

Details of the naval air activities are not easy to find in the public records. The RN seems to have been less inclined to maintain records than the RAF.

**Flying Training**

The two E & R FS units were at Rochester in 1938–39. They were probably largely civilian in nature, although a Flight Lieutenant Chambers was the CO of No.23 in April 1938. The types flown were Tiger Moths and Hawker Harts.

# Chapter 9

# AIRCRAFT CASUALTIES IN KENT
## January 1938 to August 1939

### By Ken Owen

The compilers would like to point out that the following list is unlikely to be complete and could contain errors. Any information additional to or correcting any of the items would be most welcome.

## 1938

| Date | Aircraft | Serial/ Registration | Constrs No. | Remarks |
|---|---|---|---|---|
| 20.1.38 | Gauntlet | K5310 | | 79 Squadron. Hit tractor on take off at Biggin Hill. Written off. |
| 4.2.38 | Gauntlet | K5327 | | 32 Squadron. Crashed on approach and written off at Biggin Hill. |
| 16.3.38 | Monospar ST25 Jubilee | G-AEAT | 75 | Crashed at Brasted, 8 miles NW of Tonbridge. Owned by Aerial Sites Ltd. Pilot Mr M. Willow slightly hurt, passenger unhurt. |
| 21.5.38 | Audax | K3708 | | No.23 Elementary & Reserve Flying Training School. Ditched in the River Swale near Faversham and lost. |
| 2.6.38 | Fokker Airliner | 00-AIL | | Sellindge. Crashed into Springfield House & Methodist Chapel. |

| Date | Aircraft | Serial | | Notes |
|---|---|---|---|---|
| 16.6.38 | Gladiator | K7933 | | 54 Squadron. Crashed in sea off Leysdown. Lost. |
| 30.6.38 | Hart | K3042 | | No.20 ERFTS. Overshot landing at Eastchurch and written off. |
| 6.7.38 | B.A. Swallow | G-AFGS | 483 | Crashed in sea off Folkestone. |
| 7.7.38 | Gauntlet | K5328 | | 32 Squadron. Crashed on landing at Biggin Hill. Written off. |
| 20.8.38 | Tutor | K3337 | | 23 ERFTS. Crashed in forced landing Blue Bell Hill, Maidstone — write off. |
| 22.8.38 | Tutor | K3264 | | 23 ERFTS. Crashed on landing at Rochester Airfield — write off. |
| 21.9.38 | B.A. Swallow | G-AELI | 445 | Crashed near Lympne, pilot killed, written off. |
| 21.9.38 | Anson | K8705 | | 48 Squadron. Collided on ground at Eastchurch with the following A/c written off and became 1291M. |
| 21.9.38 | Anson | K8775 | | 48 Squadron. Was run into at Eastchurch by K8705 and damaged. |
| 6.10.38 01.32 | Harrow | K6971 | | 215 Squadron. Lost in storm during tactical exercise, crashed in sea off Dungeness. Crew — F/O D.A. Hamilton, P/O T.I. Munro, A/C1 T. Prowse, A/C1 C. Lodge all missing. |
| 15.10.38 | Hind | L7236 | | 23 ERFTS. Crashed whilst landing and written off, possibly at Rochester. |
| 10.11.38 | DH60 Moth | G-ABOV | 1868 | Crashed at Crundale in fog. Pilot Jayant Pathare killed. Aircraft owned by Herts & Essex Aero Club. Was not written off until Feb 42. |
| 24.11.38 | Blenheim I | L1346 | | 21 Squadron. Undercarriage retracted on take off at Eastchurch. Damaged beyond repair. |
| 28.11.38 | Blenheim I | L1368 | | 21 Squadron. Crashed and written off overshooting at Eastchurch. |
| 3.12.38 | | | | Pilot Mr W.E. Davis killed and buried at Lympne Cemetery. |

| Date | Aircraft | Serial/Registration | Constrs No. | Remarks |
|---|---|---|---|---|
| 26.2.39 | Hurricane | L1675 | | 32 Squadron. Crashed on approach to Biggin Hill. Became 1426M. |
| 27.2.39 | Hurricane | L1782 | | 79 Squadron. Aircraft abandoned 1 mile N of Bekesbourne. Write off. |
| 4.4.39 | Hurricane | L1845 | | 79 Squadron. Crashed night landing at Biggin Hill. Write off. |
| 6.4.39 | Hurricane | L1672 | | 32 Squadron. Crashed on approach to Biggin Hill. Became 1466M. |
| 9.4.39 | Audax I | K7415 | | 20 ERFTS. Crashed Sevenoaks/Shoreham area practising low level aerobatics. The pilot P/O B.J. Sciortino was killed. |
| 17.4.39 | Anson | K8710 | | 48 Squadron. Taxied into ditch at night at Eastchurch. Damaged beyond repair? |
| 28.4.39 | Lysander I | L4702 | | 2 Squadron. Stalled and crashed at Hawkinge during slow flying demonstration. Write off. |
| 12.5.39 | Tiger Moth | N6451 | | 20 ERFTS. Crashed in Claylane Woods near Gravesend after being hit by N5487 in flight. N5487 was blamed at the subsequent inquiry. F/O F.R. Matthews & Midshipman A. Taylor both survived. |
| 12.5.39 | Tiger Moth | N5487 | | 20 ERFTS. Collided with tail of N6451 when approaching Gravesend aerodrome. F/O J.F. Spanton was killed, Midshipman C.G. Hodgkinson survived. |
| 14.5.39 | Stirling (Prototype) | L7600 | | Brake siezed, swung off runway at Rochester, under carriage collapsed and A/c written off. |
| 18.5.39 | Blenheim I | L1439 | | 25 Squadron. Crashed near Dartford and written off. |

| Date | Type | Serial | | Notes |
|---|---|---|---|---|
| 18.6.39 | Hind | K5466 | | 23 ERFTS. Crashed in forced landing at Bredhurst. Write off. |
| 20.6.39 | Tiger Moth | N5482 | | 20 ERFTS. Crashed, possibly at Gravesend and struck off charge. |
| 25.6.39 | Tiger Moth | K4287 | | 20 ERFTS. Spun into ground during solo spinning and steep turns exercise. Crashed at Rowhill Woods, Wilmington near Dartford. Sgt J.E. Morgan RAFVR killed. |
| 30.6.39 | Hurricane I | L1938 | | 3 Squadron. Spun in on approach to Biggin Hill aerodrome. Written off. |
| 2.7.39 | Gladiator | K7958 | | 615 Squadron. Crashed in forced landing Ide Hill. Written off. |
| 9.7.39 | Hurricane I | L1661 | | 32 Squadron. Abandoned 5 miles S of Herne Bay. Write off. |
| 13.7.39 | Blenheim I | L1510 | | 25 Squadron. Crashed on landing at Hawkinge. Salvaged as 1637M – Instructional airframe. |
| 21.7.39 | DH60G Gipsy Moth | G-ABJZ | 1842 | Kent Flying Club. Collided with Hawker Hind and crashed at Tilmanstone. K.K. Brown (CF Instr) & W.A. Pragnell (pupil) both killed. Written off. |
| 21.7.39 | Hawker Hind | K5418 | | Oxford Univ. Air Sqdn. Collided with the above Moth, tail of Hind cut off and crashed. Pilot D.C. Lewis killed. Write off. |
| 1.8.39 | Blenheim I | L1241 | | 25 Squadron. Overshot landing at Hawkinge and crashed. Salvaged to become Instr Airframe 1635M. |
| 9.8.39 | Hurricane I | L1557 | | 111 Squadron. Crashed after take off 2 miles SW of Biggin Hill. Write off. |
| 11.8.39 | Hurricane I | L1662 | | 32 Squadron. Hit hill in low cloud and written off near Tatsfield. Could be in Surrey. |
| 19.8.39 | | | | Aircraft crashed at Whippens Farm Borough Green. Mr E.E. Ragget aged 26 of Lord Romneys Hill, Maidstone, who was a Civil Air Guard, was killed. |

De Havilland Comet G-ACSS outside the hangars at Gravesend Airport in 1937.    (D. Kiell)

Alex Henshaw's Percival Mew Gull G-AEXF in front of a canvas Bessoneaux hangar at Gravesend Airport. (D. Kiell)

Chapter 10

# GRAVESEND AIRPORT 1938 – 39 AND THE RECORD BREAKERS

## By Ray Munday

The two years leading to the Second World War saw much activity at Gravesend Airport. The establishment and expansion of the Reserve and Flying Training School, together with some commercial and light aircraft activity saw the intensity of flying increase as the weeks went by.

The establishment of the works of the small firm of Essex Aero Ltd at the airport caused visits from some of the famous names in aviation at that time. Essex Aero came to be specialists for racing and record breaking attempts. The skill of the workers at this firm, many of them local people, caused flyers to seek the aid of Jack Cross, the Managing Director and his craftsmen in their attempts to fly faster and further. The two years followed a similar pattern with work taking place during the Winter on the aircraft to be used and the attempt on the record made in early Spring.

The first attempt in 1938 was made by Flying Officer Alec Clouston and Victor Ricketts, Air Correspondent of the London 'Daily Express'. The aircraft to be used for this attempt was the de Havilland Comet G-ACSS which had already achieved worldwide fame when in 1934 it had won the Mac Robertson England to Australia air race in the hands of C.W.A. Scott and Campbell Black. Victor Ricketts had arranged for a small shelf to be installed in the rear section of the cockpit so that he could use a typewriter to write reports on the flight whilst in the air. The intention was that his reports could be handed over at each stopping place on the flight to enable them to be telegraphed back to his newspaper. The attempt was originally made from Gravesend on 6th February 1938, but this flight came to grief in Cyprus when the undercarriage assembly collapsed after a tyre punctured whilst landing on a stony runway. The backers of the attempt arranged for Jack Cross to fly out from Gravesend to Cyprus and repair the aircraft sufficiently well to enable it to be flown back to Gravesend.

After proper repairs had been made to the Comet, the attempt on the record was made again. The aircraft had been renamed 'Australian Anniversary' for the flight, especially to commemorate the 150th Anniversary of the founding of Australia. The night of Tuesday 15th March 1938 at the airport was lit by a line of paraffin flares, placed along the line of the maximum possible length of take off. At 8 p.m. the heavily fuel-laden Comet roared down the flare path and successfully took off. The route was to be Gravesend — Cairo — Basra —

Alex Henshaw tries out his record-breaking Percival Mew Gull G-AEXF assisted by Jack Cross in a reunion at Old Warden Aerodrome, June 1978.                    (Gordon Riley)

Allahbad — Singapore — Darwin — Sydney, which the aircraft and crew eventually accomplished in spite of meeting severe heat, dense fog and torrential freezing rain en route.

When Sydney was eventually reached, vast crowds welcomed the record breakers, but for Alec Clouston the dream of flying on to reach his birthplace of New Zealand was uppermost in his mind. This presented difficulties, as the owner of the Comet had forbidden the continuation of the flight to New Zealand, but Clouston was determined in his bid to reach his homeland and, after an uneventful flight across the dreaded Tasman Sea, his goal was reached.

After a rest, the return journey was attempted and after nearly another six days the record breakers landed at Croydon Airport, which was at that time the main airport for London, having flown a total of 26,450 miles. The return journey to New Zealand had taken 10 days, 21 hours and 22 minutes, which was a new record, as were various intermediate times. During all this time the two men had a total of only 16 hours sleep.

Alec Clouston continued his career in the RAF as a test pilot during the early days of the Second World War, but managed to put in several years of operational flying with RAF Coastal Command, piloting Liberators and Beaufighters in attacks on enemy shipping. After the war he commanded the Empire Test Pilots School at Farnborough before retiring to Cornwall with the rank of Air Commodore.

Victor Ricketts, who had only piloted the Comet during spells of daylight, continued as a journalist until he joined the RAF. He became a top-line photographic reconnaissance pilot, flying de Havilland Mosquito aircraft, a direct descendant of the Comet in which he had flown on the record flight.

He gained the award of the Distinguished Flying Cross for his outstanding work photographing the targets for the bomber aircraft, both before and after the bombing, often at low level. He also toured aircraft factories during his non-flying days and gave talks to the workers, for which his earlier life in newspapers and journalism stood him in good stead. However, his luck was to run out on 11th July 1942 whilst on a photographic sortie to Strasbourg and Ingoldstadt. He was shot down and killed over Belgium, together with his Russian-born observer, Boris Lukhmanoff.

The Comet which had carried Clouston and Ricketts returned to Gravesend Airport where it was kept in the hangars until 1951, when it was refurbished for exhibition at the Festival of Britain on London's South Bank. It was then stored at the de Havilland works at Hatfield. With the merger of the de Havilland Company into the Hawker-Siddeley Group, the Comet was presented in 1965 to the Shuttleworth Aircraft Collection at Old Warden, Bedfordshire. In the early 1980s, the decision was taken to rebuild this historic aircraft for Australia's Bicentenary Celebrations in 1988 but it was not completed in time to fly again in that year.

Essex Aero Ltd were regularly entrusted with work on Alex Henshaw's racing aircraft and, with the support of his father, Henshaw determined to break the record for the flight to the Cape of Good Hope, South Africa. Henshaw chose to use his racing aircraft, a Percival Mew Gull G-AEXF, which was originally built at Gravesend. The aircraft was re-engined with a Gipsy Six Series II in place of its usual Gipsy Six R Engine and extensive major and minor alterations to the whole machine were carried out by Jack Cross and his team of engineers from Essex Aero. The modifications included the complete engine and instrument installation, alteration of the shape of the cockpit roof and wheelspats and of other details including the construction and installation of specially shaped fuel and oil tanks to fit them into the confined space in the aircraft.

Alex Henshaw left Gravesend Airport at 3.25 a.m. on Sunday 5th February 1939 and with stops at Oran, Gao, Libreville and Angola he finally landed at Cape Town at 6.59 p.m. on Monday 6th February. The return trip started from Cape Town at 10.18 p.m. on Tuesday 7th February, landing at Mossamedes, Libreville, Gao and Oran, finally landing at Gravesend at 1.51 p.m. on Thursday 9th February. Henshaw was lifted from the cockpit in an exhausted state and, after an enthusiastic welcome from the crowd waiting at the airport, he was driven away by his father to recuperate. Among the crowd was Victor Ricketts who had enjoyed the glory the previous year. The time for the return trip of 106½ hours was a new record for the journey. Henshaw and his father had prepared for the journey by surveying the route and landing facilities en route by flying a Percival Gull to the Cape in the Spring of 1938. This and the excellent preparation enabled Henshaw to complete the trip safely, although he suffered from a severe nosebleed on the return journey. The previous record for a journey had been set by Flying Officer Clouston and Mrs Kirby-Green, flying the de Havilland Comet the previous year, although the solo and single-engined best time had been set by Amy Johnson in 1936. All these aviators had connections with Gravesend, either through Edgar Percival or Jack Cross.

After both these flights, Clouston and Ricketts and Henshaw entertained Jack Cross and his team to a dinner in Gravesend and presented suitably engraved tankards to each member of the team, to commemorate their help and participation in these record flights. Later in the year, Henshaw's Mew Gull was shown to the public in Littlewoods Store in London's Oxford Street and attracted large crowds. After Jack Cross died in Gravesend Hospital on 10th September 1981, Alex Henshaw wrote an appreciation of the man and his work in 'Aeroplane Monthly' magazine and praising the work on the Mew Gull wrote, 'His advanced work on G-AEXF for the Cape records put him in a class of his own and only those familiar with the complexity of preparing a small racing aircraft to cope with vast distances, extremes of heat and cold, to operate from desert or jungle strips, can have any conception of the enormous engineering and design problems involved.'

The Mew Gull survived the war and other fates before being rebuilt completely by Tom Storey and Martin Barraclough and again flying in 1978. In June of that year, Alex Henshaw and Jack Cross were reunited together with Mew Gull G-AEXF at Old Warden Aerodrome in Bedfordshire. In the Summer of 1982 this grand aircraft flew in the air display at the Lions Air Spectacular over its birthplace of Gravesend Airport.

Although it was rumoured at the time that Alex Henshaw was planning another record attempt later in the year, again involving Jack Cross, the outbreak of war on 3rd September 1939 brought an end to civilian flying at the airport for another six years.

# Meresborough Books

17 Station Road, Rainham, Gillingham, Kent. ME8 7RS
Telephone: Medway (0634) 388812

We are a specialist publisher of books about Kent. Our books are available in most bookshops in the country, including our own at this address. Alternatively you may order direct, adding 10% for post (minimum 20p, orders over £20 post free). ISBN prefix 0 905270 for 3 figure numbers, 094819 for 4 figure numbers. Titles in print November 1989.

BYGONE KENT. A monthly journal on all aspects of Kent history founded October 1979. £1.50 per month. Annual Subscription £16.50 (£24.00 overseas). All back numbers available (some in photocopy).

## HARDBACKS

AIRCRAFT CASUALTIES IN KENT Part One 1939-40 compiled by G.G. Baxter, K.A. Owen and P. Baldock. ISBN 3506. £10.95.

BARGEBUILDING ON THE SWALE by Don Sattin. ISBN 3530. £10.95.

EDWARDIAN CHISLEHURST by Arthur Battle. ISBN 3433. £9.95.

FISHERMEN FROM THE KENTISH SHORE by Derek Coombe. ISBN 3409. £10.95.

THE GILLS by Tony Conway. ISBN 266. £5.95. BARGAIN OFFER £1.95.

JUST OFF THE SWALE by Don Sattin. ISBN 045. £5.95.

KENT CASTLES by John Guy. ISBN 150. £7.50.

KENT'S OWN by Robin J. Brooks. The history of 500 (County of Kent) Squadron of the R.A.A.F. ISBN 541. £5.95.

LIFE AND TIMES OF THE EAST KENT CRITIC by Derrick Molock. ISBN 3077. BARGAIN OFFER £1.95.

THE LONDON, CHATHAM & DOVER RAILWAY by Adrian Gray. ISBN 886. £7.95.

THE NATURAL HISTORY OF ROMNEY MARSH by Dr F.M. Firth, M.A., Ph.D. ISBN 789. £6.95.

A NEW DICTIONARY OF KENT DIALECT by Alan Major. ISBN 274. £7.50.

O FAMOUS KENT by Eric Swain. ISBN 738. £9.95. BARGAIN OFFER £4.95.

THE PAST GLORY OF MILTON CREEK by Alan Cordell and Leslie Williams. ISBN 3042. £9.95.

ROCHESTER FROM OLD PHOTOGRAPHS compiled by the City of Rochester Society. Large format. ISBN 975. (Also available in paperback ISBN 983. £4.95.)

SHERLOCK HOLMES AND THE KENT RAILWAYS by Kelvin Jones. ISBN 3255. £8.95.

SOUTH EAST BRITAIN: ETERNAL BATTLEGROUND by Gregory Blaxland. A military history. ISBN 444. £5.95.

STRATFORD HOUSE SCHOOL 1912-1987 by Susan Pittman. ISBN 3212. £10.00.

TALES OF VICTORIAN HEADCORN or The Oddities of Heddington by Penelope Rivers (Ellen M. Poole). ISBN 3050. £8.95. (Also available in paperback ISBN 3069. £3.95).

TEYNHAM MANOR AND HUNDRED (798-1935) by Elizabeth Selby, MBE. ISBN 630. £5.95.

TROOPSHIP TO CALAIS by Derek Spiers. ISBN 3395. £11.95.

TWO HALVES OF A LIFE by Doctor Kary Pole. ISBN 509. £5.95.

US BARGEMEN by A.S. Bennett. ISBN 207. £6.95.

A VIEW OF CHRIST'S COLLEGE, BLACKHEATH by A.E.O. Crombie, B.A. ISBN 223. £6.95.

## STANDARD SIZE PAPERBACKS

**BIRDS OF KENT: A Review of their Status and Distribution** by the Kent Ornithological Society. ISBN 800. £6.95.

**BIRDWATCHING IN KENT** by Don Taylor. ISBN 932. £4.50.

**THE CANTERBURY MONSTERS** by John H. Vaux. ISBN 3468. £2.50.

**THE CHATHAM DOCKYARD STORY** by Philip MacDougall. ISBN 3301. £6.95.

**CHIDDINGSTONE — AN HISTORICAL EXPLORATION** by Jill Newton. ISBN 940. £1.95.

**A CHRONOLOGY OF ROCHESTER** by Brenda Purle. ISBN 851. £1.50.

**COBHAM.** Published for Cobham Parish Council. ISBN 3123. £1.00.

**CRIME AND CRIMINALS IN VICTORIAN KENT** by Adrian Gray. ISBN 967. £3.95.

**CURIOUS KENT** by John Vigar. ISBN 878. £1.95.

**CYCLE TOURS OF KENT** by John Guy. No. 1: Medway, Gravesend, Sittingbourne and Sheppey. ISBN 517. £1.50.

**DOVER REMEMBERED** by Jessie Elizabeth Vine. ISBN 819. £3.95.

**EXPLORING KENT CHURCHES** by John E. Vigar. ISBN 3018. £3.95.

**EXPLORING SUSSEX CHURCHES** by John E. Vigar. ISBN 3093. £3.95.

**FLIGHT IN KENT.** ISBN 3085. £1.95.

**FROM MOTHS TO MERLINS: The History of West Malling Airfield** by Robin J. Brooks. ISBN 3239. £4.95.

**THE GHOSTS OF KENT** by Peter Underwood. ISBN 86X. £3.95.

**A HISTORY OF CHATHAM GRAMMAR SCHOOL FOR GIRLS, 1907-1982** by Audrey Perkyns. ISBN 576. £1.95.

**KENT AIRFIELDS IN THE BATTLE OF BRITAIN** by the Kent Aviation Historical Research Society. ISBN 3247. £4.95.

**KENT COUNTRY CHURCHES** by James Antony Syms. ISBN 3131. £4.50.

**KENT COUNTRY CHURCHES CONTINUED** by James Antony Syms. ISBN 314X. £5.95.

**KENT COUNTRY CHURCHES CONCLUDED** by James Antony Syms. ISBN 345X. £5.95.

**KENT INNS AND SIGNS** by Michael David Mirams. ISBN 3182. £3.95.

**LET'S EXPLORE THE RIVER DARENT** by Frederick Wood. ISBN 770. £1.95.

**LULLINGSTONE PARK: THE EVOLUTION OF A MEDIAEVAL DEER PARK** by Susan Pittman. ISBN 703. £3.95.

**PENINSULA ROUND (The Hoo Peninsula)** by Des Worsdale. ISBN 568. £1.50.

**PRELUDE TO WAR: Aviation in Kent 1938-39** by KAHRS. ISBN 3476. £2.50.

**RADIO KENT GARDENERS' GUIDE** by Harry Smith and Bob Collard. ISBN 3549. £3.95.

**REAL ALE PUBS IN KENT** by CAMRA in Kent. ISBN 3263. Was £1.95. Now 95p.

**SAINT ANDREW'S CHURCH, DEAL** by Gregory Holyoake. ISBN 835. 95p.

**SHORNE: The History of a Kentish Village** by A.F. Allen. ISBN 3204. £4.95.

**SIR GARRARD TYRWHITT-DRAKE AND THE COBTREE ESTATE, MAIDSTONE** by Elizabeth Melling B.A. ISBN 3344. £1.50.

**SITTINGBOURNE & KEMSLEY LIGHT RAILWAY STOCKBOOK AND GUIDE.** ISBN 843. 95p.

**STEAM IN MY FAMILY** by John Newton. ISBN 3417. £4.95.

**STOUR VALLEY WALKS from Canterbury to Sandwich** by Christopher Donaldson. ISBN 991. £1.95.

**TALES OF VICTORIAN HEADCORN** — see under hardbacks.

**TARGET FOLKESTONE** by Roy Humphreys. ISBN 3514. £6.95.

**WADHURST: Town of the High Weald** by Alan Savidge and Oliver Mason. ISBN 3352. £5.95.

**WHERE NO FLOWERS GROW** by George Glazebrook. ISBN 3379. £2.50.

**WHO'S BURIED WHERE IN KENT** by Alan Major. ISBN 3484. £4.95.

**THE WORKHOUSE AND THE WEALD** by Dorothy Hatcher. ISBN 3360. £4.95.

# LARGE FORMAT PICTORIAL PAPERBACKS

ARE YOU BEING SERVED, MADAM? by Molly Proctor. ISBN 3174. £3.50.

AVIATION IN KENT by Robin J. Brooks. ISBN 681. £2.95.

BEFORE AND AFTER THE HURRICANE IN AND AROUND CANTERBURY by Paul Crampton. ISBN 3387. £3.50.

THE BLITZ OF CANTERBURY by Paul Crampton. ISBN 3441. £3.50.

EAST KENT FROM THE AIR by John Guy. ISBN 3158. £3.50.

EAST SUSSEX RAILWAYS IN OLD POSTCARDS by Kevin Robertson. ISBN 3220. £3.50.

GEORGE BARGEBRICK Esq. by Richard-Hugh Perks. ISBN 479. £4.50.

HEADCORN: A Pictorial History by the Headcorn Local History Society. ISBN 3271. £3.50.

KENT TOWN CRAFTS by Richard Filmer. ISBN 584. £2.95.

THE LIFE AND ART OF ONE MAN by Dudley Pout. ISBN 525. £2.95.

THE MEDWAY TOWNS FROM THE AIR by Piers Morgan and Diane Nicholls. ISBN 3557. £4.95.

MORE PICTURES OF RAINHAM by Barbara Mackay Miller. ISBN 3298. £3.50.

THE MOTOR BUS SERVICES OF KENT AND EAST SUSSEX — A brief history by Eric Baldock. ISBN 959. £4.95.

OLD BROADSTAIRS by Michael David Mirams. ISBN 3115. £3.50.

OLD CHATHAM: A THIRD PICTURE BOOK by Philip MacDougall. ISBN 3190. £3.50.

OLD FAVERSHAM by Arthur Percival. ISBN 3425. £3.50.

OLD GILLINGHAM by Philip MacDougall. ISBN 3328. £3.50.

OLD MAIDSTONE'S PUBLIC HOUSES by Irene Hales. ISBN 533. £2.95.

OLD MAIDSTONE Vol.2 by Irene Hales. ISBN 38X. £2.50.

OLD MAIDSTONE Vol.3 by Irene Hales. ISBN 3336. £3.50.

OLD MARGATE by Michael David Mirams. ISBN 851. £3.50.

OLD PUBS OF TUNBRIDGE WELLS & DISTRICT by Keith Hetherington and Alun Griffiths. ISBN 300X. £3.50.

OLD SANDWICH by Julian Arnold and Andrew Aubertin. ISBN 673. £2.95.

OLD TONBRIDGE by Don Skinner. ISBN 398. £2.50.

PEMBURY IN THE PAST by Mary Standen. ISBN 916. £2.95.

A PICTORIAL STUDY OF ALKHAM PARISH by Susan Lees and Roy Humphreys. ISBN 3034. £2.95.

A PICTORIAL STUDY OF HAWKINGE PARISH by Roy Humphreys. ISBN 328X. £3.50.

A PICTUREBOOK OF OLD RAINHAM by Barbara Mackay Miller. ISBN 606. £3.50.

REMINISCENCES OF OLD CRANBROOK by Joe Woodcock. ISBN 331X. £3.50.

ROCHESTER FROM OLD PHOTOGRAPHS — see under hardbacks.

SMARDEN: A Pictorial History by Jenni Rodger. ISBN 592. £3.50.

THOMAS SIDNEY COOPER OF CANTERBURY by Brian Stewart. ISBN 762. £2.95.

WEST KENT FROM THE AIR by John Guy. ISBN 3166. £3.50.

Published for the Kent Aviation Historical Research Society by Meresborough Books, 17 Station Road, Rainham, Kent. ME8 7RS.

Meresborough Books is a specialist publisher of books on Kent, including several on aviation. Those in print at the time of going to press are listed in the back of this book.

**KAHRS OFFICERS**
Chairman — Roy Humphreys
Secretary — Ken Owen
Treasurer — Robin J. Brooks
Archivist — David G. Collyer

ISBN 0948193 476

Printed by Staples Printers Ltd, Rochester, Kent.